COLLECTING ANTIQUE TOOLS

Herbert P. Kean & Emil S. Pollak

Photographs by Laurie Davis

Line drawings by Herbert P. Kean

D1604753

The Astragal Press
Morristown, New Jersey

Published by
The Astragal Press
P.O. Box 338
Morristown, NJ 07963-0338

Book design by Charles Lada
Manufactured in the United States of America

Library of Congress Catalogue Card Number 90-70725
ISBN 0-9618088-5-3

First Edition

TABLE OF CONTENTS

INTRODUCTION

Man's ability to make and use tools differentiates him from all other animals. It is the basis for our society, with its material and social benefits. Take away our tools and we would revert back thousands of years.

Our emphasis in this book is on woodworking hand tools that were made and used during the last few hundred years. Our point of view is that of the collector. We have particularly concentrated on those tools that are affordable, available, and interesting. We illustrate and describe over 700 of the more important varieties. We have tried to organize this material in a logical and easy-to-use format, and to make our descriptions clear, avoiding excessive technical detail and jargon. We have made a special effort throughout the book to point out potential pitfalls.

We discuss how and where to go about acquiring tools and what determines their value. We describe ways to clean, restore, preserve, and display your tools. We list clubs and societies you might wish to join and worthwhile books you may wish to read or use for reference.

Drawing on our own experience and that of others, we have tried to make your collecting as rewarding and problem-free as one can in a book.

Those who have never worked with wood may feel that they are at a disadvantage in collecting tools. Not so. Woodworking skill is not necessary. Appreciation is all that's required.

The collection and study of antique tools is a relatively recent development, and interest in the field shows strong, steady growth.

It's easy to understand why.

Many who collect are tool users, professionals and amateurs. They often find that antique tools provide higher quality than their modern counterparts and cost less. Many craftsmen simply enjoy the "feel" of older tools and a sense of kinship with the early craftsmen who once owned and used them. There are a number of contemporary woodworkers who insist on using tools of the period, when they work on restorations or reproductions.

Some of these tools are homemade primitives, reflecting the hardscrabble make-do world of their owners; while others, with fine finishing and detail and sophisticated design, reflect quite a different world. But in nearly all cases we find an individuality and pride of workmanship which, together with the ingenuity and endless variety of the tools, make collecting them a fascinating pastime.

For many, collecting antique tools is a way of experiencing history. Handling and studying these early artifacts, some of them hundreds of years old, takes us back in time. Who were these owners and makers whose names are so often found on the tools? When and where did they work? How did they live?

Many of us also collect antique tools for their aesthetic qualities: the beauty of the materials used, their designs, shapes, and proportions. Sometimes the appeal is in their utter simplicity and functionality; other times their intricacy and detail are dazzling. Many of the early mass produced tools share these qualities.

There is also the matter of economics. Antique tool prices are low compared with most other collectibles. The total proceeds from a 600-lot major tool auction are usually less than those realized from the sale of a single canvas painted by a recognized American impressionist.

For us collecting has meant all of the above: the pleasure of using fine old tools, the sense of history they impart, their beauty, the fun of finding and restoring, the interesting people we have met and the friends we have made, the knowledge we've acquired, and the information that we've shared.

This book is a result of that experience. It is about antique hand tools and how to collect them.

We hope you will enjoy the collecting experience as much as we have. It has been a joy for us and something that we wished to share.

Collecting Antique Tools was made possible by the efforts of many people. We would like to thank Laurie Davis and her staff at Fototronics for the excellent photography and processing; Chuck Lada for the design and layout of the book; Martyl Pollak for her efficient and dedicated support in editing and typesetting.

We are especially grateful to the group of experts who reviewed our work on the various tool categories, making many valuable suggestions:

❀ Ron Pearson, author of *A Guide to American Brace Patents 1829-1910*, who reviewed the section on boring tools.

❀ Paul Kebabian, author of *American Woodworking Tools* and many articles, who reviewed the section on edge tools.

❀ John Whelan, author of a forthcoming major reference work on the history and types of wooden planes, who reviewed wooden planes.

❀ Roger K. Smith, author of *Patented Transitional and Metallic Planes in America 1827-1927*, who reviewed the metal plane section.

❀ Philip Stanley, editor of the periodical *Mensuration* and author of *Boxwood and Ivory: Stanley Traditional Rules 1855-1975*, who reviewed measuring devices.

❀ Dan Comerford, co-author of *The Hammer*, who reviewed the hammer section.

❀ Frank Kingsbury, editor of *The Tool Shed*, who reviewed the section on wrenches.

BORING TOOLS

The need to bore a hole in a piece of wood has always been part of woodworking. Bored holes, used with wooden pegs, served to join pieces of wood, whether in a post and beam building or a table top. Smaller bored holes were used to help start a nail or a screw, preventing splitting and making the job easier. A bored hole would permit a keyhole saw or a fret saw the necessary room to start a cut for a lock or a decorative design. For the wheelwright, holes were needed to set the spokes, and for the cooper, the spigot. The need for boring tools was basic and the uses endless.

We have divided boring tools into three major categories: drills, augers and reamers, and braces. The drill bits used in these tools are covered at the end of this chapter.

DRILLS

BOW DRILL

The bow drill is one of the few tools that we can document as far back as ancient Egypt and which continued to be used through Greek and Roman times and into the 19th century. Simple examples are still being used in third world countries. Its principle is simple. It is propelled clockwise, then counterclockwise, by a bow, with its thong looped around the spindle, moving back and forth, in much the same way that American Indians used to start a fire.

Two early 19th century examples are shown in Fig.1. In some cases, each drill bit used was fixed in its own pad, which was then taper-fitted into the spindle or stock. In other instances the bit slipped directly into the drill or was fixed.

There are some 19th century bow drills, usually English, that combine the highest workmanship and the finest materials. They often have ivory spindles, rosewood (or sometimes ivory) handles, and brass fittings. These, of course, command premium prices. Seldom do you find an original bow that matches the drill, and many bow drills are sold without any bow at all. Bows seem to have been lost or discarded. If you decide to replace a missing or improper bow, your best starting material is the blade of an old fencing foil.

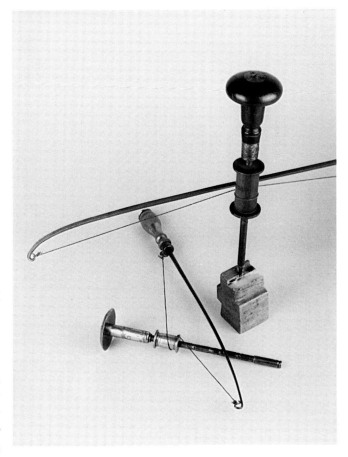

Fig. 1   Two early 19th century bow drills.

PUMP DRILL

The reciprocating pump drill is simple but fascinating. It's a challenge to see how long you can keep it going. The thong, or string, is twisted around the shaft by turning a crossbar (Fig.2). Then downward pressure on the bar spins the shaft until the thong is retwisted in the opposite direction. This cycle continues over and over, almost like a child's toy. The flywheel, originally wood, iron, or stone on the more primitive models (this too is a very ancient tool), was changed to brass during the 19th century.

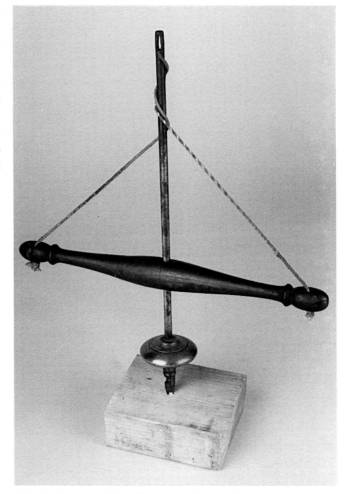

Fig. 2 A pump drill with a brass flywheel.

ARCHIMEDEAN DRILL

The archimedean drill is a much more modern tool than those previously mentioned. It works by vertical reciprocating movement of the lower wooden grip, which spins the spiral worm of the shaft: clockwise then counterclockwise. The drills shown in Fig.3 are examples of late 19th century manufacture and were often used as screwdrivers as well as drills. They are forerunners of the "Yankee" and then Stanley reciprocating screwdrivers used even today.

Fig.4 shows more sophisticated types that were used in Victorian times for fine work, sometimes by dentists or by jewelers. The examples shown use a fly wheel or extended weights to increase and maintain velocity.

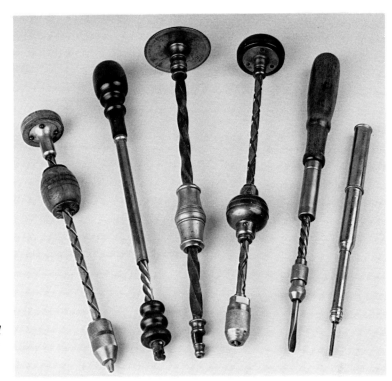

Fig. 3 Six archimedean style drills. The first four from the left operate by moving the grip up and down; the last two are pushed. These drills were sometimes used as screwdrivers, as shown by the example second from right..

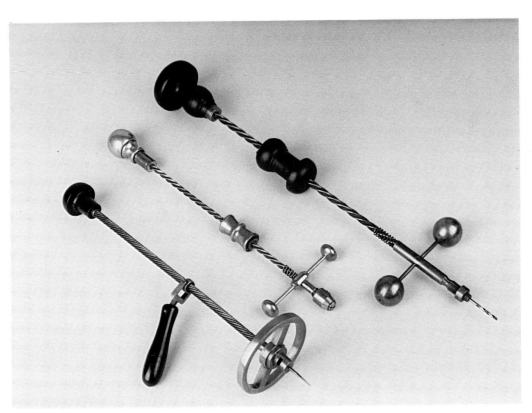

Fig. 4 More sophisticated archimedean drills, used for fine work.

BEVEL-GEARED DRILL

The idea of being able to turn a drill bit rapidly in one direction was realized in the development of the geared drill in the early 19th century. Throughout the next 100 years, improvements were made to allow for varying speeds, both forward and reverse; breast plates, to apply body pressure; levels, to keep the drill plumb; removeable handles, to permit varying uses; and a variety of chuck styles, to hold the bit firmly and to allow bits to be easily changed. It is a tool that is still used when power is not available on the job site (Figs. 5 through 8).

Drills are still available at low cost to the collector in a fascinating and seemingly endless variety.

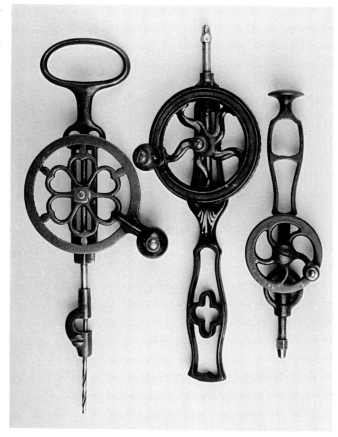

Fig. 5 Examples of early hand drills.

Fig. 6 Two mid-19th century bevel drills. The one on the left has its extension shank removed and shown alongside it.

Fig. 7 A beautiful craftsman-made breast drill.

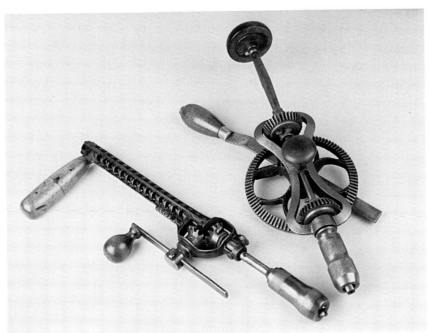

Fig. 8   Two patented drills: left, the Rusby patent with its extendable shank; right, a ratchet action made by the Int'l. Mfgr. Co., Worcester, Mass.

AUGERS and REAMERS

AUGER

Augers are most often simply boring bits with an attached cross-handle, forming a T-shape (Fig.9). They are used by pressing downward into the work and turning the handle clockwise. The larger augers required great manual effort, some needing two men to turn them.

Although augers date back to at least the 10th century, most were made after the origin of the twisted bit (1770). Every farmer and woodworker had a set, and consequently they are still common and inexpensive today. The blacksmith-made spiral augers were produced by heating a piece of pre-shaped iron and twisting it to form the spiral flutes that were the forerunners of the modern twist drill. These early handmade flutes were not perfect in their spacing, and can easily be distinguished from the later more perfectly formed factory-made augers. The spiraling served to remove the chips, particularly from deep holes where they would otherwise choke and bind the bit. Earlier types, such as the nose auger and the spoon auger (see section at end of chapter) required the bit to be brought out of the hole periodically to clear the chips.

Very small augers, used mostly for starting holes, are called gimlets. Most have screwtips that pull the bit into the wood. Some are of the shell type and some spiral (Fig. 10). The heaviest of the gimlets were used for boring holes for spikes in ship's timbers, while some of the longest were used by bell hangers to run string for household bells, and later by electricians to run wire through walls.

Although an auger collection may include many different types of bits, the greater interest lies in the different methods of attaching the bit to the handle. The original technique was merely bending over the tang (or shaft) of the bit as it came through the handle. Later, the tang was threaded and locked to the handle with a nut. There followed a number of patented augers, improving the method for attaching the bit to the handle and providing for easy release and the use of various sized bits.

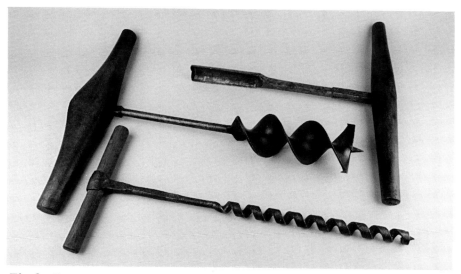

Fig. 9 *T-augers: upper right, a nose auger; the other two, spiral augers.*

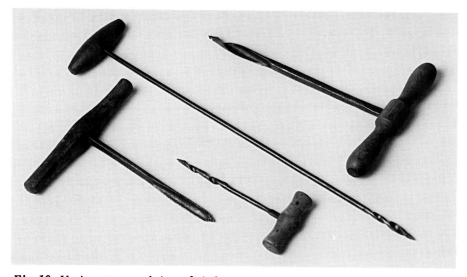

Fig. 10 *Various types and sizes of gimlets.*

A little known fact is that most early waterpipes in major cities were wooden. New York City's original mains (dating from the early 19th century) were logs a foot or more in diameter with 3" - 5" holes drilled through their centers with augers. These pipe augers consisted of a bit attached to a 12 to 16 foot iron rod and turned by an iron T-handle. The style of these early bits were mostly nose (see end of chapter), which worked well in end-grain. Smaller pipe augers were used for pipes that transported water from the pump to the user, and these were called pumplog augers.

The most interesting of all the augers is the beam boring machine (sometimes called a barn borer, Fig.11). Its name describes its use. Most all holes used for starting mortises in post and beam construction were drilled first with augers and then chiseled out. The beam borer had the advantage of continuous rotation, since it was geared. It did not, however, have the necessary leverage and downthrust for large holes, but depended on the pull of the bit. Some of these machines could tilt, i.e. drill at an angle to the beam, and many had rack gears for easier upward bit removal. Most had wooden frames, some were made entirely of metal, and there were patented models as well. Altogether a fascinating piece of Americana.

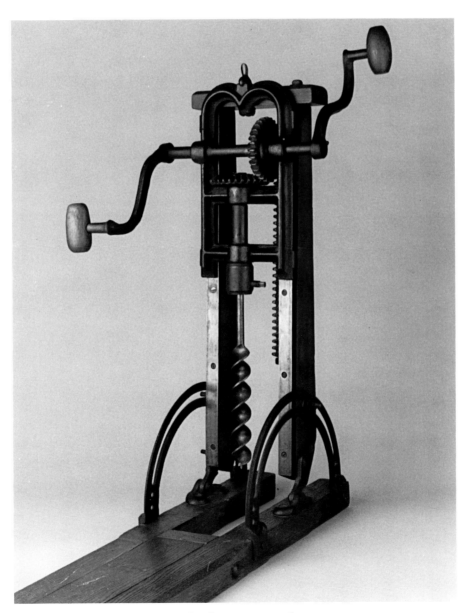

Fig. 11   A boring machine used in heavy construction.

REAMER

Reamers are tools that look very much like side- cutting tapered augers (Fig.12). However, unlike augers, reamers have no tip mechanism to start the hole. They are used to enlarge an existing hole, to create a tapered fit, or to reduce the amount of effort needed, by not having to cut the hole to final size on the first pass. Coopers, wheelwrights and pump log makers all used reamers for these reasons.

The larger reamers, particularly those used by wheelwrights, are dramatic in their workmanship. They are artforms of hand- forging. Many of these have hooks at their tips, the speculation being that a large weight was hung on this hook after the reamer was inserted into the starter hole in the wagon hub. This would help provide the downward centering thrust needed to cut the large deep hole. Another theory (not held by us) is that the hook was merely for hanging up the tool, since most of these very large reamers had removable handles.

Pipe and pump log reamers are similar to the pipe augers except, as with all reamers, they do not cut with their tips, but with their sides *only*. Once the hole was opened with the auger, the graduated set of reamers was used to enlarge its diameter. The pipe logs themselves fit together by matching internal and external end

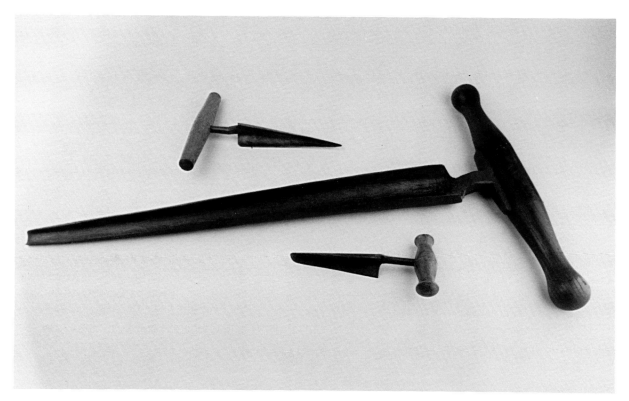

Fig. 12 *Reamers: in the center is a wheelwright's reamer; the other two are cooper's reamers.*

tapers. The female (internal) end was cut with a heavily tapered reamer, while the male taper was cut with a tapered rounder called a Turk's Head (because of its resemblance to a Turkish turban). Sets of these pipe log tools, augers, reamers, handles, and turk's heads, are most valuable when complete and original, but original sets are rare and most collectors are satisfied with representative examples.

The early cooper used a reamer to cut the bung hole (for the cork) in the barrel. Later the reamer was fitted with a starting screw tip and it made its own hole and brought it to size, all in one operation (Fig.13). This latter tool is called a bung hole borer.

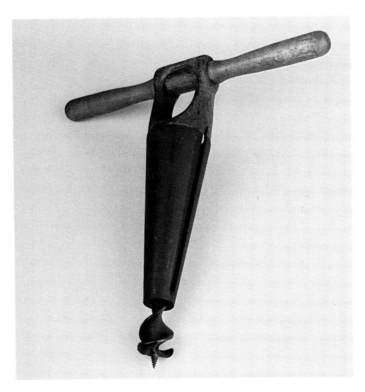

Fig. 13   A cooper's bung hole borer, showing both the boring tip and the reaming sides — a combination of the two tools.

BRACES

It seems strange, considering how simple its concept and how great its utility, that the brace was among the last of the boring tools to be developed (probably originating in the 15th century). Besides being very useful, it is also one of the most visually pleasing of the tools and offers the collector a fascinating variety. Most of the early braces were made of wood, a material less expensive and more readily available than iron or steel. Later versions were improved by reinforcing points of strain with brass plates. Finally, by the mid-19th century, the wooden brace was superseded by mass-produced metal versions, though many of these later braces continued to use wood for head and grip, utilizing wood's superior comfort and appearance.

PRIMITIVE BRACE

Fig.14 is a sketch of an early wooden brace identifying the various parts of the brace that we'll be referring to as we go along.

The basic wooden brace changed very little over the centuries. Braces seen in 15th and 16th century paintings are nearly identical to the 18th century American braces shown in Fig.15. A note of caution: because many traditional tools such as braces have changed little over the years, collectors should be very wary of attribution of age based solely on appearance.

Primitive braces were made in a number of basic shapes, reflecting regional styles and country of origin, but were often modified to suit the preferences of the maker or the requirements of the work being done. Braces with a tilted grip are most often Scandinavian in origin, while German and Austrian braces of later vintage (they were made well into the 20th century and almost always of hornbeam) have more elaborate

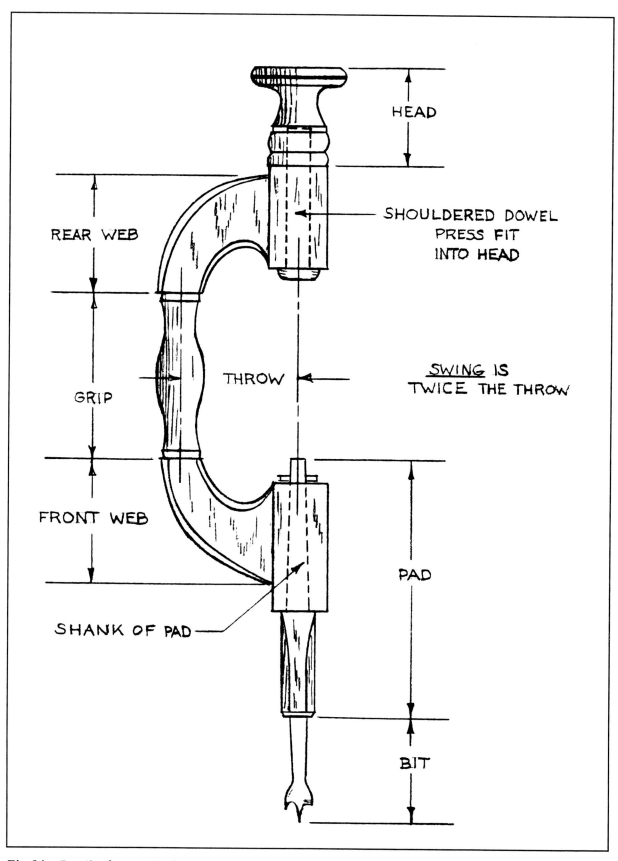

HEAD

SHOULDERED DOWEL
PRESS FIT
INTO HEAD

REAR WEB

THROW

SWING IS
TWICE THE THROW

GRIP

FRONT WEB

PAD

SHANK OF PAD

BIT

Fig. 14 *Details of a primitive brace.*

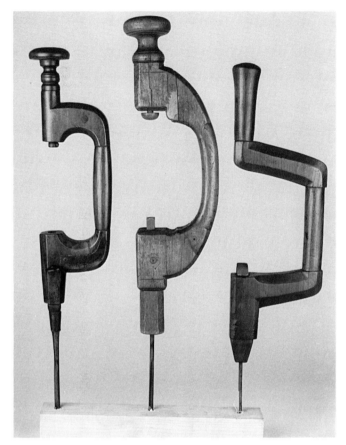

Fig. 15   *Three early American wooden braces.*

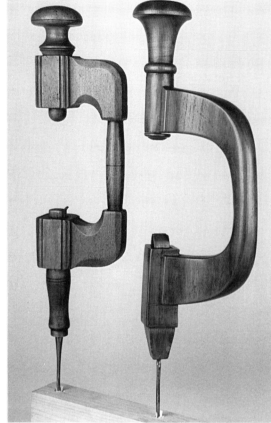

Fig. 16   *Two European braces: to the left Austrian, right Danish.*

turnings and beadings (Fig.16). Those with slanted rear webs (Fig.17) are more the style of the Dutch. Earlier braces tended to be handcarved with a continuous arc to the grip (the center brace in Fig.15). Those where the maker had the advantage of a lathe generally had a turned grip (braces on the right and left in Fig.15). The width of the web was determined by the amount of stress that the brace was to receive. Braces used to start holes in softer woods had narrow webs in comparison with the ones used for boring oak, ash, and hickory, or used in heavy work by wheelwrights, housewrights, or shipwrights. Regardless of usage, braces probably also varied in web thickness depending on how many times the maker had a brace crack on him. Primitive braces from all parts of Europe are frequently found in the United States, brought here by immigrant artisans or made here in the traditional style of their homeland.

The part of the brace that continued to change over the years was the method of holding the bit. It is believed that originally the bit was permanently fixed into the stock (hence the name bitstock). However, it was a reasonable evolution to develop a brace that could hold bits of different sizes and kinds and one in which worn bits could be replaced. As the tangs of the bits were not yet standard, the workable thing was to use a "go-between" or pad as it was called. The pad permanently received the bit and was, in turn, made to fit the brace hole. Almost all of the tangs on these pads were square to prevent spinning, and tapered to "lock in." The locking-in didn't always work. Many braces show the addition of a thumbscrew to grip the shank of the pad in a positive way. For a higher degree of positiveness the shank was pinned through with a removeable pin.

It is indeed a valuable brace that has all its original pads and bits. Examples have been found with up to 14 original pads but this is extraordinary. Most collectors are happy with one original. As there is considerable difference in value between an original pad and bit and one that has been replaced (no matter how properly), it pays to learn how to recognize the difference. Shape, wood and patina are the three best criteria. The maker usually extended the geometry of the brace into the pad, so if the nose of the brace was hexagonal or square, the pad generally followed suit. The chamfering was also carried from brace to pad. In almost all cases, the wood used was the same species. But the acid test is the patina. Patina, the finish achieved by years of use, is hard to duplicate, and only the very skillful can achieve a good match. Most don't even try, and the mismatch is easily spotted.

An interesting device that eliminated the need for a perfect pad taper or a cross-pin, yet still prevented the pad from slipping from the brace when it was reversed out of the drilled hole, was the "clothespin" tang. It is a split tang that is forced together going into the brace, and springs back to lock the pad in when the extensions on the end of the tang clear the web (Fig.18). These pads are considerably rarer than the standard solid type.

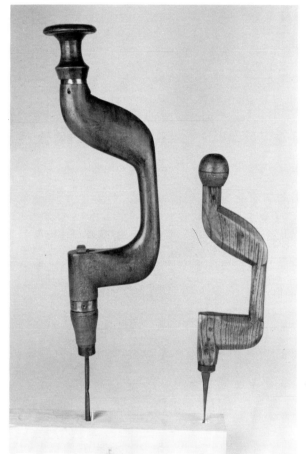

Fig.17   *Two Dutch braces (called spykeboors).*   **Fig.18**   *The "clothespin" tang.*

The wood used for these early braces was predominantly beech, but birch, maple, apple, ash, and even hickory and oak were also used. The exotic woods, i.e., rosewood, ebony and boxwood, appeared in later manufactured braces. So if you see a gorgeous primitive brace of rosewood or ebony, the likelihood is that you are looking at the product of a later-day woodcrafter.

Many of the heads of these braces have worn at the juncture to the stock, through years of downward pressure. Throughout this book, there are times when repair or restoration is recommended. This is one of the times when it is not, even though it is not difficult. Any repair of this nature would result in the brace appearing contrary to its natural look. We have yet to find a worn primitive brace with a tight original head.

If the heads were broken, they were replaced, but they weren't fixed if they could function "as-is," a philosophy used in management today: "If it ain't broke, don't fix it."

While on the subject of retaining a brace's "proper look," we want to emphasize that cleaning an 18th century brace could destroy the wear-pattern patina that is so appropriate and traditional with these early braces. Until you truly know what you're doing, refrain from cleaning primitive braces.

Old braces frequently show evidence of early repair — most often where stress created splits in the webs or the lower stock where the pad was inserted. These repairs allowed the brace to continue to perform and eventually survive its maker. Friendly controversy between collectors often centers on whether this added "character" increases or diminishes value. Part of the answer often depends on whether you are the buyer or the seller. We believe that early repairs, when well done, can add to the appeal of a piece and give it authenticity and individuality.

CHAIRMAKER'S BRACE

This is one of the few braces that continued to use fixed bits over the centuries without change. We can only suppose that chairmakers, who worked in permanent shops and didn't have to carry their tools around, could accommodate the extra braces. They probably found the rigid fixed bit more accurate to work with, and not having to find and change bits a convenience (Fig.19). Each brace was fitted with a different size bit, generally of the spoon or shell type (see end of chapter). They were used to drill the holes to mate with the tenons in the stretchers, rungs, and backs of chairs. They were also used to drill holes for pegging in the seatboards.

Fig. 19   The chairmaker's brace.

The chairmaker's brace had a comparatively small head and was often used with a breast bib, a piece of hardwood shaped to the chest, secured with a strap, and having an indentation that received the head of the brace. This allowed the workman to apply body pressure and additional guidance. These bibs are very seldom found.

Chairmaker's braces are quite graceful and finely made. They reflect the high degree of skill required of the chairmaker, since, in most cases, he made his own braces. This skill can be even more appreciated when we consider some of the great masterpieces of chairmaking that were created using these imprecise and difficult-to-handle tools.

All of these braces had iron or brass ferrules around the nose, to keep the pressure of the bit from splitting the stock. Many of the ferrules are missing today, detracting from the value of the brace.

Almost all chairmaker's braces were made of beech, though applewood was sometimes used. These rarer applewood examples are the more desireable.

COOPER'S BRACE

Coopering, or barrelmaking, was an extremely important craft in earlier days. Every town had at least one cooper, and the cooper was an indispensable crew member of every whaling ship, assembling barrels to hold the sperm oil. Similarly tobacco plantations employed coopers to make hogsheads in which to ship the dried leaves. Even today barrels are used to age wine and whiskey. Picture in your mind how many things are packed in corrugated cartons or plastic, glass, or metal containers and you'll get some idea of the necessity of barrels in earlier days. As late as the 1890's there were over 50,000 cooperages in the United States. Barrels came in a great variety of sizes, some almost room-size.

Whether "wet" (tight barrel cooperage) for liquids, or "dry" (slack barrel cooperage) for produce, hardware, and other non- liquid bulk, the role of the cooper's brace was solely to match boards in the head (or lid) by blind doweling. The cooper would drill into the edge of the head boards at matching positions and

Fig. 20   The cooper's brace.

insert the dowels. Presto! he had a laminated board wide enough to saw out the complete diameter of the head. Barrelmaking required a tough rugged individual and the cooper's brace reflects this characteristic. The heads are larger than those on any other brace, as they were most often used against the body, so the cooper could work the brace with one hand and hold the board with the other (a neat trick - try it some time). (Fig.20).

The bit was forced between tight-fitting iron jaws, which could be knocked out from the back side when the bit needed replacement. Some braces will be found with these jaws missing, and the bit permanently wedged into the stock itself. As with the chairmaker's brace, ferrules were used to keep the bit from splitting out the wood, and a good percentage of the time the ferrules are missing. These defects reduce the value of the brace for the collector.

SHEFFIELD-STYLE BRACE

18th and 19th century Sheffield, England, was a world-renowned center for the manufacture of steel and tools. It exported to all corners of the world and, in many instances, produced a quality that still surpasses that achieved in the automated production lines of today. Some of the most beautiful tools ever produced were made in Sheffield.

The Sheffield brace (Fig.21) was basically a standardized and improved version of the wooden brace, mass produced by the Sheffield tool makers.

Although the style started in the late 18th century and was made all but obsolete by the iron braces of the late 19th century, hundreds of thousands of these braces were made, many of which have crossed the Atlantic. The stocks are almost always beech, with the heads most often lignum vitae. There are a number of variations that fall into three categories:

1. While some examples are plain and unadorned, many have brass stiffening plates on the webs that strengthened and prevented cracking, and also provided decoration. This style was added during the early part of the 19th century.

2. A brass chuck was used that held and released the bits by depressing a button. However, some models used levers and, in a few rare cases, had rings similar to those in the ultimatum style (see next section). In purchasing a Sheffield brace be sure that the button, lever or ring is there, and actually holds the bit. The value of the brace is substantially diminished without this feature.

3. The necks of most models are wood which is generally part of the head. The more expensive models, and today more valuable, have brass necks and usually ebony heads.

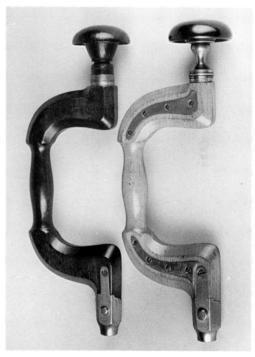

Fig. 21 Two Sheffield braces; the right plated, the other unplated..

In some cases the brass disks in the head (called trade disks) will show a different maker from the name stamped on the brass chuck. Don't despair, you may not have a replaced head. Many craftsmen in those days specialized and sold heads to the stockmakers (those who made the bodies), the most prolific headmaker being Henry Brown. However, replacement heads were also regularly sold. Most often they were in two pieces, screwed together. Because of this separation, access was available to disassemble the head without need for a hole in the end (the very hole which was covered by the brass trade disk). So if you have a brace with a head that does not have a brass disk or a wooden plug in it, you probably have a replacement head.

Many Sheffield braces have worn heads with consequent wobble. The 19th century craftsmen had a quick way to correct this. They merely removed the head and stuffed a small piece of leather (or a washer) between the spindle locking nut and the head. Modern day restorers do exactly that, with excellent results.

Novice restorers sometimes replace the screws in the brass plates with brass screws. Sounds logical, but it's incorrect. All the manufacturers used steel screws.

On rare occasions you may find a Sheffield brace with the stock made of an exotic wood, e.g., ebony, rosewood, or boxwood. This brace could be as much as ten times more valuable than one made of beech.

A few of the many maker names you might find on a Sheffield brace are listed below:

James Bee	D. Flather & Sons	Robert Marples	A. Mathieson	Joseph Slater
Henry Brown	James Howarth	Marsden Bros & Co.	Moulson Bros.	
Fenton & Marsden	Thomas Ibbotson & Co.	Marsh Bros.	Henry Pasley	

ULTIMATUM-STYLE or BRASS FRAMED BRACE

The ultimatum brace (Fig.22) was just that, the ultimate brace and the ultimate expression of English Victorian toolmaking. It was produced at a time, mid to late 19th century, when the British Empire was at its zenith, London was the financial center of the world and Sheffield steel and tools synonymous with the best. Ultimatum braces were made to be used in the same sense as a Rolls Royce was made to be driven. With their heavy shining brass frames contrasting with the ebony infill and the ivory ring inset in the head, and costing the equivalent of a week's wages for a workman, they symbolized success. The very fact that they were more for show than for use has allowed many of them to survive for present day collectors to own and admire.

These brass-framed braces were made with an iron spindle (through the grip) which was peened onto the front and rear brass frames. The frames were "filled" with blocks of wood carved to fit, and screwed to the frames.

The infill was most often ebony, followed in

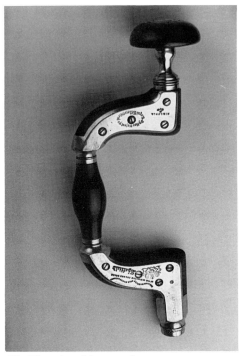

Fig.22   An ultimatum brace.

order of rarity by beech and rosewood, with horn and boxwood the rarest of all. Most had ivory rings in their heads, surrounding the trade disk. Many of the beech models had no rings, or had the ring grooves cut but nothing in them (beech was supposedly used as a fill-in when the factory couldn't complete the order in ebony). The only other exception to the ivory ring is the boxwood model which carries an ebony ring in a boxwood head.

As with the Sheffield-style braces, the chucks used either button, lever or ring to secure the bit, but the latter was by far the most common. The necks were always brass. Many years ago, tool collectors realized that the name "Ultimatum" did not apply to all brass-framed braces, even though they looked alike. Kenneth Roberts, a foremost authority on brass-framed braces, resolved the question in his book *Some 19th Century English Woodworking Tools.* He pointed out that only William Marples and Robert Marples (in the mid- and late-19th century) produced braces with the inscription "Ultimatum" on the side plates; and only William Marples' braces were allowed to be inscribed "By Her Majesty's Royal Letters Patent." All others, e.g., Ross, Turner, Ridge, Slack, Wilson, etc. were copies of William Marples' design made specifically for the "trade" (and known today as trade braces), or independently made under different patents and registries, e.g., Flather, Marsden, Sorby, Howarth, Pasley, etc.

This doesn't imply that William Marples' braces are the most valuable. In truth there are more of his braces around than those of any other signature. But, because he was one of the first, and held the Queen's Letters, and because they had the word "Ultimatum" on the side, his braces tend to be more valuable than most trade braces. There are, however, many makers listed in Roberts' book that command even higher prices.

Although the construction of the brass-framed brace was designed to be the ultimate in braces, there was a problem with its assembly. More often than not, the peened joints loosened and the brace rocked on the grip. This is one of the points to look for when purchasing a brass-framed brace. A wobbly head can be repaired per suggestions given under Sheffield braces. Even the many chips and checks generally found in ebony can be filled for more pleasing aesthetics. But the rocking grip is best left alone. Unless it is severe, it does not decrease the value appreciably.

As many of the ivory rings have been replaced over the years, it pays to check to be sure all the ring is there and that it is intact.

A word of caution if this is your first ebony tool. Ebony is very susceptible to heat and dryness. Sometimes just being in the back of a car exposed to the hot sun will cause checks and could loosen the ivory ring. A collector friend of ours was unaware that the humidifier in his home malfunctioned until he noticed cracks in all his ebony pieces. A sad day for both him and his insurance company.

HANDFORGED BRACE

As iron and steel became less expensive and more available, many woodworkers turned to blacksmith-made braces, preferring their greater durability over wood. By the end of the 18th century there were nearly as many different forms of handforged braces as there were blacksmiths. The variety is endless (Fig.23) but almost all had three things in common:

    1. The grip and stock were one piece.

    2. There was an enlarged nosepiece with a tapered square hole to hold the bit.

    3. There was a revolving head, generally of wood with a strengthening ferrule at the neck.

As the bits were rarely held by friction alone in the "chuck," a screw was generally added. Some of these have elements of folk art with descriptive names like wing screw, heart screw, ram's horn, and rat tail. Sometimes these screws have either broken off or have been lost through the years, reducing slightly the value of the brace.

Many of these rudimentary braces are gracefully formed and beautifully decorated with chamfering and file work. They are magnificent examples of the blacksmith's art (Fig.24).

Cage head (lantern or squirrel cage) braces (Fig.25) are a subgroup of handforged braces, but have a greater sophistication in the unique mechanics of the head, which is supported with bars or rods coming together at the neck. This structure allows much heavier downward stress while boring, without the subsequent bearing wear and wobble.

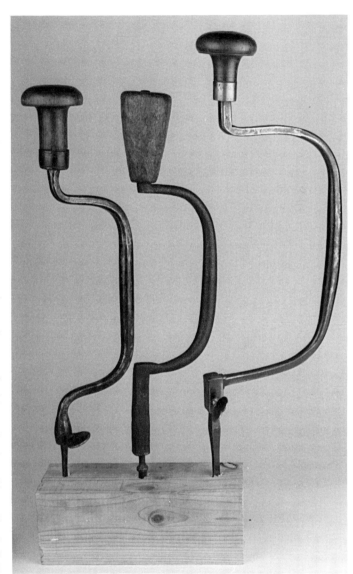

Fig. 23 Three examples of early blacksmith-made braces.

The bars resemble the bars on a cage; hence the name. Known examples have between two and six bars. The rarity, and thus the value of this brace, tends to increase with the number of bars. Though made for, and given, heavy use, many have survived.

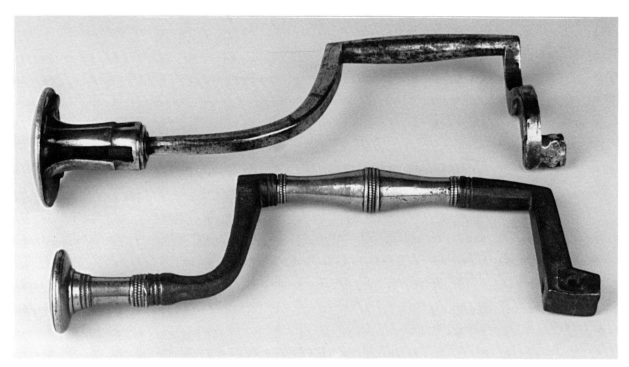

Fig. 24 *Two early decorated braces, probably European.*

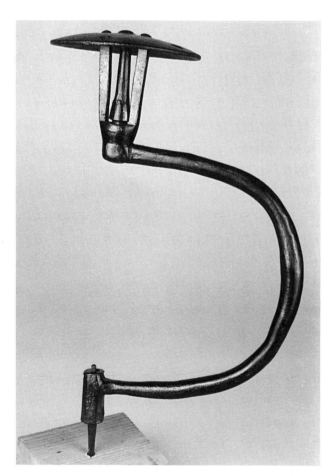

Fig. 25 *A two-bar cage head brace.*

GENT'S BRACE

This was among the earliest of the standardized, mass produced iron braces, first appearing in the early 19th century. It had a variety of names in addition to Gent's: sixpenny brace (the price for which they sold in England around 1900), ball brace, common brace, German brace, thumbscrew brace, cheap brace (Fig.26).

Its one significant difference from the blacksmith brace was the revolving ball on the grip. This made for a better feel and fewer blisters. As the ball was made in two halves and then assembled around the grip with nails and glue, many have come apart and been lost or broken. Often they will be found held together with wrapped wire. Produced in great quantity, these braces are still plentiful today, and examples missing the ball or otherwise damaged have very little value.

The name Gent's or Gentlemen's Brace seems amusing in a way. One wonders what the

Fig. 26 The Gent's, or sixpenny, brace.

advertiser was trying to convey. Was he trying to tell the consumer that this was the "aristocrat" among iron braces, or that the brace was designed and made for the use of "gentlemen"? Whichever, this style brace was produced and sold by the millions for over a century, and probably used for light work, whether by gentlemen, amateur woodworkers, or as an extra in the woodworker's chest. One version, whose head folded into the throw, was made for undertakers. Carried in their pockets, it could be quickly assembled, fitted with a screwdriver bit and used to close the coffin after the viewing. Surviving examples are rare and much sought after by collectors.

WAGON BRACE

Toward the latter half of the 19th century, the efficiency of the iron braces became apparent to everyone. They could be used to bore through difficult woods without fear of breaking. They could be dropped, run over, kicked or thrown in anger. They were almost indestructible. The wagon brace was used for such heavy work in the wagon shop as the boring of the various pegging and mortising holes. Wagon braces tended to have a deeper throw which gave the user greater leverage, as can be seen on the Fray patented brace with a Spofford-style chuck (Fig.27).

The cheaper variety had a metal head, while the better wagon brace retained the wooden head. Both the wing screw and the lever were used in the early models, later changing to the Barber chuck (see American Braces).

Fig. 27 The Spofford chuck on a Fray patent brace.

The Scotch brace was an elegant variety of the wagon brace, with its bulbous grip, hexagonal body, top lever chuck and a brass ferrule on a wooden head (Fig.28).

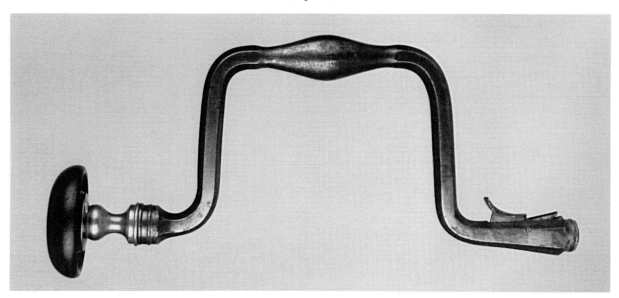

Fig.28   The Scotch style wagon brace.

AMERICAN BRACE

Yankee ingenuity soon over-took and then dominated the brace production of the world. By the late 19th century, American metal braces with various patented chucks, such as the Spofford and the Barber, had become so popular that all other types were disappearing. American braces were advertised in English, Dutch, German and Austrian tool catalogs. No longer was Sheffield, England, the "King of Tools."

During this period it seemed as though everyone had an idea on how to improve the brace and proceeded to patent it. Over 400 brace patents were issued in the United States in the 19th and early 20th centuries, offering today's collectors a tremendous variety to collect and study (Fig.29).

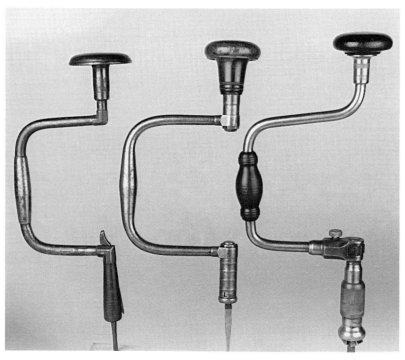

Fig. 29   American manufactured braces. From left to right: Taylor patent; brace manufactured by Charles E. Staples, Worcester, MA, ca.1860; and Davis Level & Tool Co. patented May 25, 1886.

Fig.30 shows a few of the many different styles of patented chucks that were offered in the marketplace. As with the automobile industry, where 1500 companies finally ended up as the big three, only one of the hundreds of patented chucks has survived to this day: the ratchet variety of the Barber chuck (Fig.31).

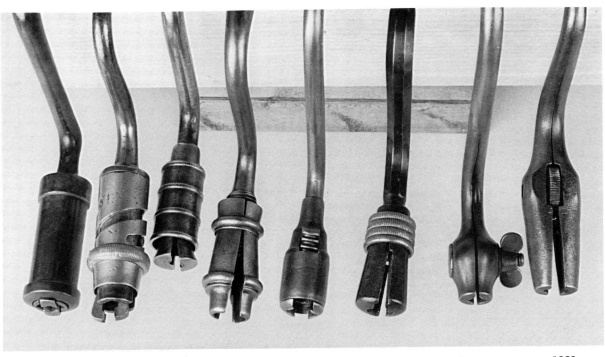

Fig. 30 *Some examples of 19th century patented chucks. From left to right: (1) Felix Chantrell patent, 1882 (rare); (2) G.L. Holt patent, 1880; (3) G. Stackpole patent, 1862; (4) H.S. Shepardson patent, 1870; (5) Milton V. Nobles patent, 1865; (6) C.W. Daboll patent, 1868, mfd. by Wilson Mfg. Co.; (7) Stackpole patent, 1867; (8) Royall S. Hildreth patent, 1870, mfd. by Athol Mfg. Co.*

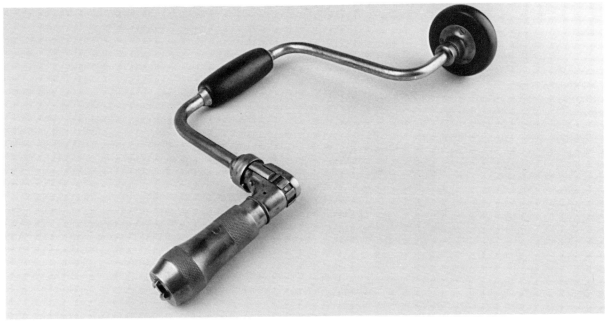

Fig. 31 *The most successful patented chuck, the Barber patent, shown on a Millers Falls brace, circa 1890.*

BITS

In comparison with the beauty and mechanical ingenuity of the brace, the bits themselves have tended to be treated as "plain janes," simply the cutting edges of the tool. Yet bits show an interesting transition over the years, from blacksmith forged to machine manufactured, and a great variety of types and sizes. There are really only three major categories (Fig.32):

1. Hollow bit - with its varieties of:
   a. spoon - the tip is enclosed like a spoon.
   b. shell - the tip is open. (Also called gouge or quill.)
   c. nose - the tip has a flat cutting spur.
   d. reamer - the body is tapered.
2. Center bit - has a centering point and one edge spur, cutting a circumferential slice, and the other side removing the wood chip with a flat cutter.
3. Spiral bit - early bits had only one spiral flute and one cutting edge. Later types developed the double spiral that is predominantly in use today.

There are also many special bits: screwdriver, spanner, gimlet, countersink, washer cutters, etc. (Fig.33). Two more complicated bits are the spoke pointer and the tenon cutter. The spoke pointer has the blade on a slant to the work and consequently puts a point or chamfer on spokes and other dowels for ease of assembly and fit (Fig.34). The tenon cutter has the blade at right angles to the work and cuts a smaller diameter "tenon" on the tip of the spoke or chair leg for a shouldered fit to the drilled hole in the mating piece. It has sometimes been referred to as a hollow auger. Some models have adjustments for size of dowel, depth of cut, and position of blade (Fig.34).

Although it is not difficult to display a full set of bits, as they lend themselves to mounting on boards, there is no better place for them than in the very braces they were designed to work with, enhancing the beauty and form of the brace itself.

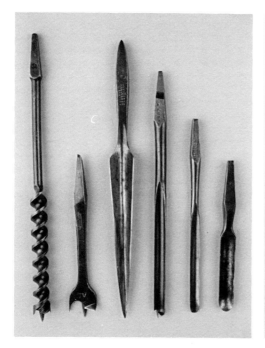

Fig. 32   A variety of bit types. From the right, spoon, shell, nose, reamer, center and spiral.

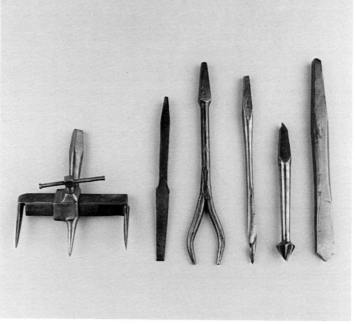

Fig. 33   Other interesting types of brace attachments: from left, washer cutter, screwdriver, spanner, gimlet, countersink, blacksmith.

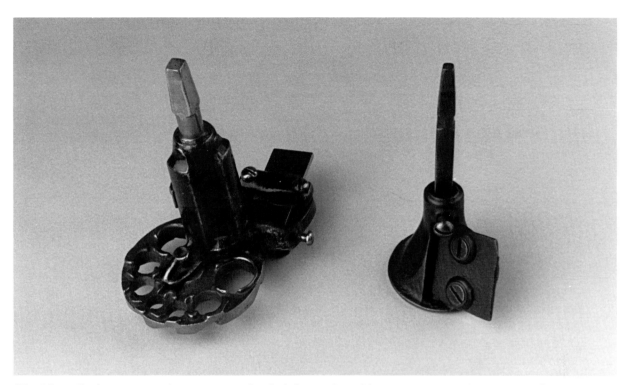

Fig. 34   *Spoke pointer and tenon cutter. On the left, an adjustable tenon cutter; on the right, a spoke pointer.*

EDGE TOOLS

Tools that cut must have an edge of some sort. We shall, however, follow the traditional definition of the edge tools and confine this section to axes, adzes, chisels and knives, leaving boring tools, saws, and planes, all of which have cutting edges, to their own separate categories. We'll put the remaining tools with edges such as taps and screw boxes in the "other tools" category.

Edge tools are among the earliest tool forms, with surviving primitive axes dated to 8000 B.C.

American pioneers, facing vast tracts of virgin forest, knew the importance of the axe and held nothing but their rifles in higher esteem. Even at the start of our modern era, the boast of a good woodsman was that all he needed to survive in a wilderness area was "two matches and an axe."

AXES

Early axes were made by "wrapping" the red hot iron around a form, yielding the eye of the axe. The steel bit, introduced in the 18th century, was laid into the fold at the front and hammered into an edge. The side opposite the bit was later extended into a poll, for better balance and to provide a hammering surface (Fig.35).

Handles took on a variety of shapes, some indicative of origin, others relating to function. The length of the handle, although many times tailored to the size of the man, had more to do with the arc of the swing that was required. Felling axes, used with great impact, took a full swing and therefore needed the longest handles.

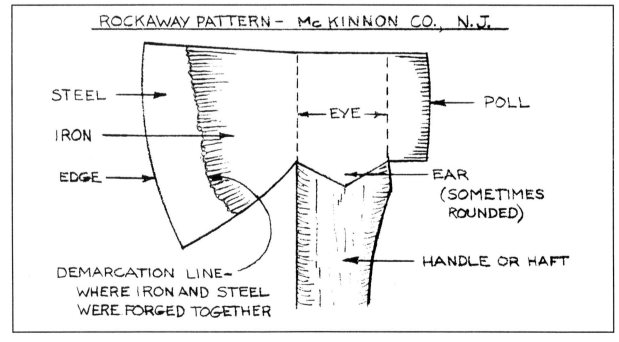

Fig. 35 *Details of an axe. Steel was not used in axes until the mid 18th century. Iron was no longer used after the late 19th century. However, demarcation lines can still be seen on some 20th century axes, as two types of steel were forged together.*

Early axes have their handles fitted through the eye from the top down and the handles remain in place by locking into the taper of the eye, so they can be removed for sharpening. Good reason to handle these axes with care. (Adzes also work on this principle).

Later axes, however, have their handles fit through the eye from the bottom up, and have a wedge driven in from the top. This permanently locks the handle to the axe and was much preferred by American woodsmen. Naturally, there was the inconvenience of replacing the handle when broken, but these men quickly learned how to cut the handle off directly under the eye and drive it back out.

Many axes found today had been discarded because the handle was split or broken off. In most cases they can be bought at a fraction of their value and, with another handle and a little effort, restored to their original condition. Most axe collectors have a stock of older flea-market handles (new ones just don't look the part) that they use for this restoration. Like plane blades, axe handles might have been replaced two or three times throughout the life of the tool. One more replacement won't detract that much from its value, as long as it is "proper," i.e., the right shape and length for its function.

In most comprehensive books on tools, axes are the first tools discussed. Maybe it's just alphabetical, but we like to think it's because they are such a basic tool and have contributed so much to the development of civilization.

SINGLE BIT FELLING AXE

The workhorse of the axe family is the single bit felling axe (Fig.36). It is simple in design, varying from a 2½ lb. head used by campers to the 4½ to 7 lb. head used for forest work. There are heads seen in lumbermen's competition up to 12 lbs. but these are rarely used on a day to day basis. With the advent of the two-man crosscut saw, and later the power chain saw, trees no longer are felled by axes (although the lower cut, called the undercut, is sometimes cleared out with an axe). The axe is more a utility tool for clearing branches off the downed tree, driving wooden wedges to relieve the tension of the sawcut, and splitting firewood. There are a great number of shapes to the head, each woodsman preferring the type common to his area.

Fig. 36   Single bit felling axes.

DOUBLE BIT FELLING AXE

Only skilled woodsmen use the double bit axe (Fig.37). The balance of this axe is better than that of a single bit, and there is an advantage to keeping one edge sharp for felling and using the other for "swamping-out," i.e., clearing brush and branches in preparation for "bucking," (cutting the downed tree into logs.) However, the safety hazard for the novice is all too apparent; he has a blade facing him on the backswing.

Double bit axes always have straight handles, unlike any other modern axe. Almost all axe handles are hickory. Hickory has both strength and spring, and was found very early to be the best for axe handles. Old time woodsmen do complain that the quality of the handles is not what it used to be — but what is?

Starting in the late 1800's a number of axe manufacturers adopted intricate logos that were embossed or etched on the head of the axe. Almost 200 different styles have been identified to date and these have also become an interesting collectible.

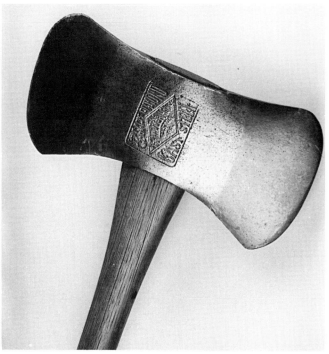

Fig.37   *Double bit felling axe with the embossed trade mark.*

BROAD AXE

Not as common as the felling axe, and a lot larger (ranging up to 9 lbs.) is the hewing or broad axe (Fig.38). Its purpose was to square up logs into beams. It was used with a much shorter swing than was used with the felling axe, and therefore required a much shorter handle. The identifying feature of many of these axes is the chisel edge (one-sided bevel to the edge) that allowed the back side of the axe to be dead flat. But this posed a problem of clearance for the hands. To keep the hands from being scraped, the handle was canted or swayed away from the flat plane of the axe. This is a feature that should always be looked for when buying a broad axe. If the edge is chisel-sharpened (basiled), then the handle should be swayed. And the swaying should be such that if the axe lays on its flat side, the end of the handle should be up 3" — 4" above the blade. If the handle is upside down, it can be taken out and turned around. If there is no sway to the handle, it is improper.

Fig. 38   *Two styles of broad axes. On the left is a Pennsylvania pattern; right, a Canada pattern. Both have their handles set into the heads for left-handed use.*

The disadvantage to this swayed configuration is that from any given side it can only be used in one direction down the log. This is not always easy if the grain is"running out," i.e., not truly longitudinal. So most woodsmen who hewed steadily preferred to have two broad axes, a left-handed one and a right- handed one. It's easy to get them mixed up. Visualize the log on the ground and you on the left side looking up the log, with the blade in a vertical position. If the flat side of the blade fits against the left side of the log, as it would when cutting, then your axe is left-handed. If you were on the right side, with the blade vertical and flat, the axe would be right-handed.

To get away from the difficulty of swaying or canting the handle and also from having two axes, some broad axes were sharpened from both sides (knife-edged) and had straight, longer handles. They were used for such work as hewing railroad ties and mine timbers, where hewing to a perfectly straight line was not quite so important.

As with the felling axe, the broad axe heads have a variety of patterns, again mostly a result of geographical preferences. Fig.39 shows some of the more common styles in this country.

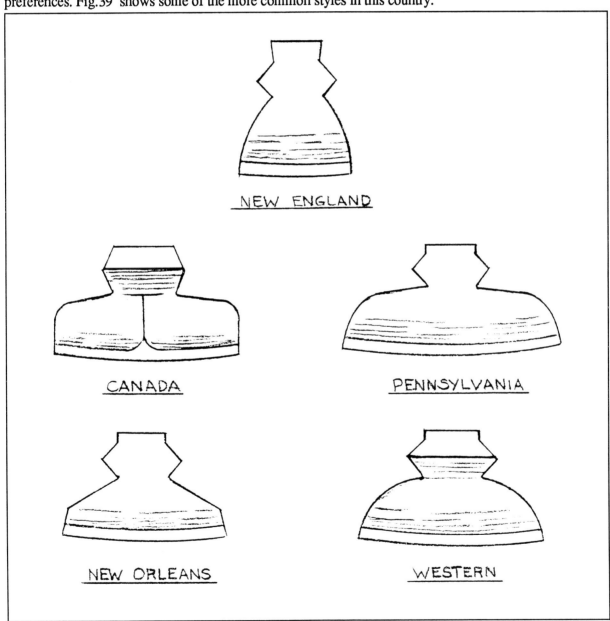

Fig. 39 Broad axe patterns.

GOOSEWING AXE

One of the most dramatic and artistic looking tools is the goosewing hewing axe (Fig.40), which takes its name from its resemblance to the wing of a goose in flight. It functions exactly as the chisel-edged broad axe, except that the American version has the handle socket more heavily bent or canted up from the plane of the blade. As such, the handle could be straight, yet still yield the necessary hand clearance.

These axes are large (up to 15" edges) and difficult to forge. Many show cracks and repairs. An original handle is rare. Signed pieces, particularly by American makers (mostly Pennsylvania Dutch), are considerably more valuable.

The problem is in being able to recognize a contemporary or World War II vintage axe from the 18th or 19th century ones. Also of importance is the difference in value between American and European axes, the American ones being worth considerably more. A few well-known 19th century American makers whose names appear imprinted on axes are Stohler, Stahler, Sener, Rohrbach, Addams, and L. & I.J. White. Important American characteristics are: narrower eyes, under ⅜" wide; few, if any, decorative imprints; more heavily canted sockets; narrower polls, under ¾" across; and a grainy "charcoal" iron. These characteristics are not "written in stone," because many times the maker brought his skills from the old country. Fig.41 shows typical American and European style differences.

Contemporary axes do not have the laid-in edge, and have a very smooth finish to the steel. The reproductions (for decorator use only) have almost broomstick handles with burned aging and no edge to the blade. If you look closely, you can see the acetylene welds and power grinder marks.

Take care in handling a goosewing or any old axe. The handle was usually friction-fit to the head and time has probably loosened the fit. Don't hold the axe by its handle with the head down. Always hold these old axes by the head.

Fig. 40 Goosewing axes . Left: European style; right, American style.

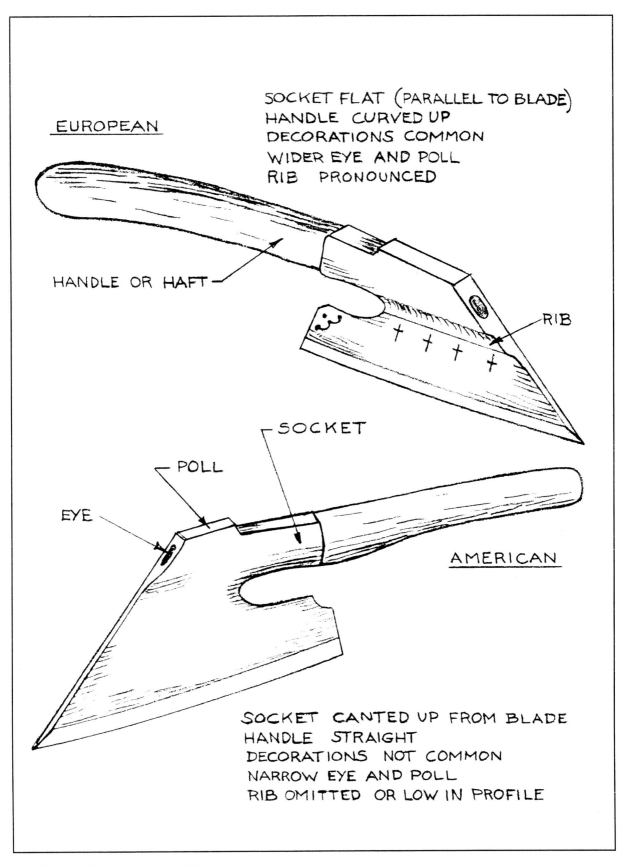

EUROPEAN

SOCKET FLAT (PARALLEL TO BLADE)
HANDLE CURVED UP
DECORATIONS COMMON
WIDER EYE AND POLL
RIB PRONOUNCED

HANDLE OR HAFT

RIB

SOCKET

POLL

EYE

AMERICAN

SOCKET CANTED UP FROM BLADE
HANDLE STRAIGHT
DECORATIONS NOT COMMON
NARROW EYE AND POLL
RIB OMITTED OR LOW IN PROFILE

Fig. 41 Details of American and European syle goosewing axes.

SHIPWRIGHT'S or MAST AXE

Used for shaping ships' masts and timbers, this axe is usually ground on both sides, and varies in length based upon local usage. The double pointed ears or lugs are common with this axe (Fig.42).

Fig. 42   Shipwright's, or mast, axe.

COOPER'S AXE

The cooper's axe has a lighter handle socket, well canted, and carries a very short handle. Although the general differentiation between an axe and a hatchet is that an axe is used with two hands and a hatchet with one, the cooper's axe is one of the exceptions to the rule. As it was used mostly for shaping barrel staves, it was almost always used with one hand while the other held the stave. Fig.43 shows the most common shape.

Fig. 43   Cooper's axe.

COACHMAKER'S AXE

This is an asymmetrical axe used for shaping coach parts in almost a paring manner. The heads vary in size, some styles taking on a "bearded" effect, hence the nickname "bearded axe." These axes are almost exclusively of European origin (Fig.44).

Fig.44   Coachmaker's axes; bearded axe, left.

ICE AXE

Not too long ago ice was harvested in the winter from ponds and lakes and stored in ice-houses for summer use. This was an important winter cash crop for many a farmer. There was a whole family of tools developed to serve this industry, among them the ice axe.

Once again, local patterns create a variety of styles. One of the most common models is shown in Fig.45. Its usage is easy to visualize. The long narrow blade chopped the ice blocks apart, while the rear pike moved the blocks around. As these were used only to cut ice, they rarely had laid-in steel in their bits.

Fig. 45   Ice axe.

FIRE AXE

These are sought-after collectibles, as many of the older ones have the fire company's monogram on the head. All have rear pikes used for "pulling down," i.e., to clear openings or create ventilation. Fig.46 shows an early axe.

Fig. 46   Fire axe.

MORTISING AXE

The blade on these axes are long and narrow to accommodate the size of the mortise hole it was designed to cut, most often for post and beam construction or for post and rail (Fig.47). Some have double bits; one bit sized for the length and the other for the width of the hole.

Fig. 47   Mortising axes.

TRADE AXE

Trades axes were originally brought over by the French and Spanish and later by the English and were traded to the Indians who held them in very high regard. They were poll-less and small enough to be carried at the belt and used with one hand (Fig.48). The larger variety were known as squaw axes and were used by the women for chopping wood. There are a good number of similar-appearing axes that have come over from Spain in recent years; they have been cast rather than handforged. These examples are less desireable, and can be differentiated from the hand-forged ones by their absence of a slight lap where the blade comes together after wrapping around the eye. Be careful that what you acquire is truly a part of America's past.

Fig. 48 Trade axes. On the left is a squaw axe; on the right a belt axe.

TURF or BOG AXE

Used for cutting turf and peat, these axes are not heavy enough to cut wood. Fig.49 shows two models.

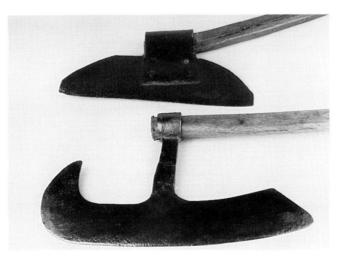

Fig. 49 Turf, or bog, axes.

HATCHET

Hatchets are small axes used with one hand. Shown in Fig.50 is a lathing hatchet used for nailing up narrow strips of wood and then wire prior to the plastering of a wall. Fig.51 shows both a general utility and a camper's-type hatchet.

Fig.50   Lathing hatchet.

Fig.51   On the left, a utility-type hatchet, often used for shingling. On the right, a camper's hatchet.

ADZES

The adze has approximately the same historic lineage as the axe. It has traditionally been used for shaping and flattening boards and timbers wherever the axe was awkward to use and the plane did not remove enough wood, for example in house framing and building the decks of ships. The bevel of the blade is always on the "inside" (the side curved toward the handle), making sharpening difficult unless the head can be easily removed. Thus, almost all adze handles are taper fit into the head of the adze, generally through a rectangular hole, and can quickly be separated from the blade.

Old seaman could always tell who was the ship's carpenter. He was the one with one or two toes missing. Even though the swing of the adze was controlled by locking one arm against the thigh, the adzeman still worked with the blade striking dangerously close to his feet.

Like axe handles, almost all adze handles are made of hickory. The interesting curve in the longer handles make them pleasing "wall-hangers." A good explanation for some of the more exaggerated curved handles doesn't appear in any of the literature. We can only guess that the owner wanted the blade in the best position to protect his feet.

CARPENTER'S ADZE

The most common adze that the collector will find is the carpenter's adze. Some are poll-less, some have block-like polls, and some have octagonal or round extensions to their polls (Fig.52). In addition to leveling floors, beams, and rafters, the carpenter could do shaping work with this tool in a more controlled fashion than with the axe.

SHIPWRIGHT'S ADZE

These adzes were either "lipped" (rolled up edges) or flat (Fig.52). More control and a smoother cut was gotten with the lipped style. In either case, the poll had a spike-like extension, which was used for "setting" (driving below the surface) any nails or obstructions. The ship's carpenter used his adze for any shaping work on timbers, masts, spars etc. and for levelling of the deckboards.

Fig. 52 On the left a shipwright's adze; in the center and on the right carpenter's adzes, poll-less and polled, respectively.

GUTTER or HOLLOWING ADZE

This tool is almost self explanatory. Its hollow cutting head was used to scoop out the troughway of early gutters and other similar concavities (Fig.53). Usually blacksmith forged, it is rarer than the carpenter's adze.

Fig. 53   Different examples of gutter, or hollowing, adzes; all blacksmith made and therefore quite individual.

HAND ADZE

As their name implies, these adzes, described below, were used with one hand, in a similar way to a hatchet. Although there are many varities, the three listed below are the most likely to be found by the collector. They are generally rarer and therefore more valuable than the longer two-handed adzes.

STIRRUP, SPANISH, or STRAP ADZE

Originating in the Roman era, this style adze was prevalent in Spain and Portugal right up to modern times. Most had open handles, but others had the closed "D" handle (Fig.54). The D-handled adzes are sometimes called "Connecticut type" and represented to be early American, for reasons not clear to us. The blades used were often imported from Sheffield, England, and therefore have Sheffield makers' marks. The tool was, however, used primarily by Spanish and Portugese artisans.

COOPER'S ADZE

The cooper's adze was used to bevel the ends of barrel staves in preparation for the lid. Early cooper's adzes were handforged and had handles that were fitted into rectangular holes in the head. Later factory models had a long bolt through the handle with a nut at the very bottom. This facilitated the removal of the blade for sharpening. Almost all cooper's adzes have a hammer-head style poll, as the polls were used to pound down the hoops that held the barrel together (Fig.55).

If you find a cooper's adze with a nut (or any obstruction) on the head end, it is either put together incorrectly or has improper replacement parts. The top surface of the head must be smooth all the way to the poll, or else any follow-through of the stroke would gouge the work.

BOWL ADZE

Used for gouging out bowls, etc., this adze has a hollow head similar to the gutter adze. In many cases, the handle is tilted forward so as to "wrap" the blade around the fist (Fig.56). This provides excellent control and allows almost paring action for the final cut. Some of the widest adzes are bowl adzes, ranging up to 9" in width!

Fig. 54 Stirrup adzes. Left, closed handle; right, open handle.

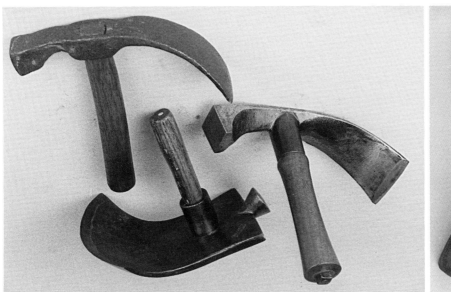

Fig. 55 Cooper's adzes. Upper left, handforged; center, the French style; right, factory-made.

Fig. 56 Bowl adze.

CHISELS

Chisels, like the previous edge tools, date back to the Stone Age. However, unlike the axe and the adze, chisels have maintained their importance up to the present. In some applications they are the most important tools in the woodworker's chest. There are dozens of sizes and variations of each configuration, amounting to literally hundreds of individual models. Although some styles of chisels do not incorporate the word "chisel" in their names (e.g., gouges and slicks), we will consider our general discussion of chisels to include all types.

The chisel is a rather simple device composed of a blade that shanks into a wooden handle, or has the handle fit into the blade's tapered socket. A ferrule generally protects the end of the shank-fitted handle from splitting. A ring is used on the back end of both types if pounding with a mallet is anticipated. Modern chisels that have their shanks cast in plastic have no need for ferrules or rings. These plastic- handled chisels are very usable but not yet considered as collectible. Chisels and gouges were also made from old files.

Chisel handles are usually turned (some are octagonal) with many differences in patterns, based upon the trade they are intended for or the styling of the manufacturer. The more common ones are made from beech, ash, maple or hickory, while the finer ones are boxwood or rosewood. Although the grade of steel is the most important measure of a chisel, the handle is what makes it visually appealing.

FIRMER, FRAMING, or STRAIGHT CHISEL

The square-ended, flat firmer chisel is the simplest and most common of all chisels. It is thick enough to be pounded and used for heavy work, although sometimes its sides are beveled thin to work corners better (Fig.57).

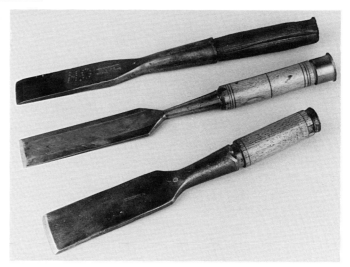

Fig.57   Firmer chisels.

PARING CHISEL

These are longer, thinner and more delicate chisels that pare the wood without being struck with a mallet. As such, they have no pounding rings. Some have their shanks bent for hand clearance. These "crank-necked" models are sometimes called patternmaker's chisels (Fig.58).

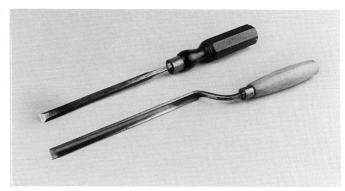

Fig.58   Paring chisels.

-38-

GOUGE

A gouge is a U-shaped chisel varying from almost flat to semi- circular, utilizing a variety of radii. Most have their sharpening bevel (cannal) ground on the outer surface of the U, and are called out-cannal ground. Those required to cut with the blade more parallel to the work are ground on the inside surface and are called in-cannal ground (Fig.59).

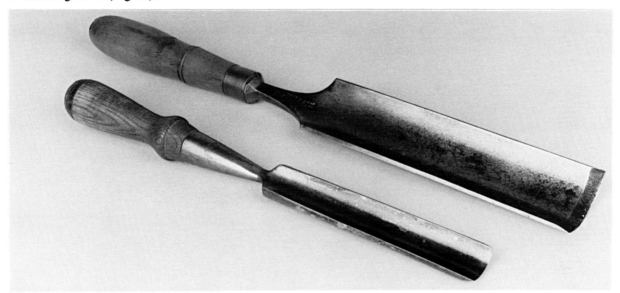

Fig. 59   *Gouges. Top, in-cannel; bottom, out-cannel.*

MORTISE CHISEL

One of the most popular joints in fine woodworking is the mortise and tenon. It consists of a rectangular hole (the mortise) in one piece and a similar shaped male section (the tenon) in the mating piece. A common method of making the mortise is by drilling holes and squaring up the sides and corners with mortise chisels. Fig.60 shows the standard mortise chisel, and the gooseneck (or lock) mortise chisel that allows for pivoting leverage in deep joints. Fig. 61 shows the corner chisel (sides at a 90° angle);and Fig. 62 shows the bruzz or wheelwright's corner chisel (sides at approximately a 60° angle). The rare French twybill, which was as long as 48", was gripped by the socket, and used as a paring chisel to clean out the mortise. The American version has a much shorter blade and usually was fitted with a handle.

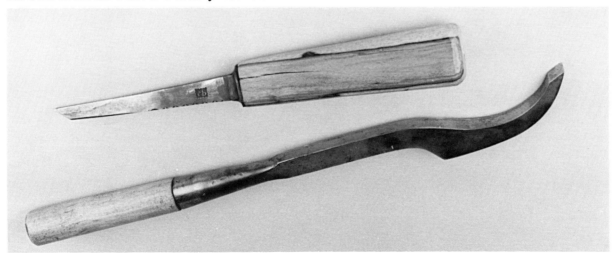

Fig. 60   *Mortising chisels. The standard style above; the goose neck below.*

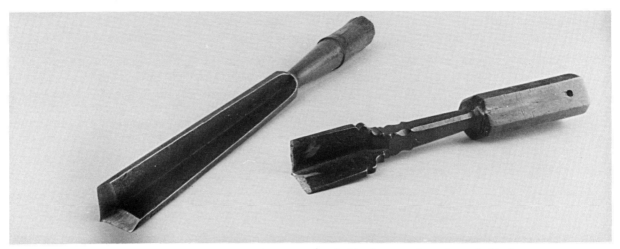

Fig. 61   Corner chisels. The example on the right is a very early file-decorated continental chisel.

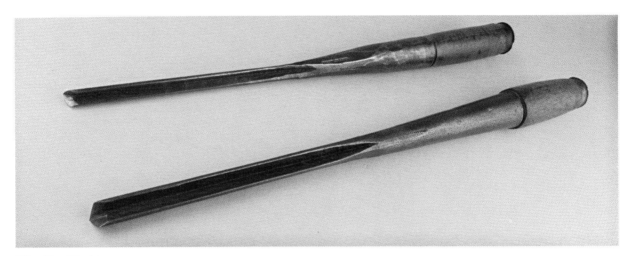

Fig. 62   The bruzz.

SLICK or SHIPWRIGHT'S CHISEL

This tool was used mostly to shape heavy timbers; its blade ranged from about 2" to 4" in width. The handle was gracefully turned with a palm grip or rounded end. It was fitted into the tapered socket of the blade. As this chisel was never struck, merely pushed, it did not have a pounding ring. One other feature that differentiated the slick from a large firmer chisel, or an ice chopper, was the tilt upward of the slick's handle, to give hand clearance (Fig.63).

Fig. 63   Slick.

TURNING TOOLS

Turning tools are used with lathes to turn rounded parts of furniture, posts, etc. They generally come in sets of eight, although professional turners have far more. The set consists of flat skews (end sharpened at a diagonal), gouges, scraper, vee chisel, and a thin parting tool (Fig.64). If repetitive work is to be done, the turner's sizing tool (Fig.65) is set to cut narrow grooves to various diameters. This series of grooves gives the turner a base line for the freehand turning of the contour.

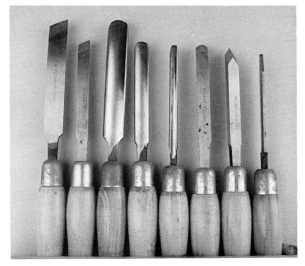

Fig. 64 Turning tools.

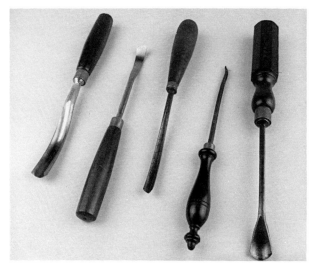

Fig. 66 Carving tools.

CARVING TOOLS

The largest number of chisels and gouges usually is found in the carver's chest, as artwork requires an almost infinite variety. These tools are smaller than most, and are predominantly of the gouge type. Skews and V-shapes are common, however. Some special forms of gouges are (a) spoons (blades curves in two dimensions like a spoon), (b) fluters (deeper than than regular gouges), (c) veiners (higher sides to the U-shape than the fluter) and (d) the macaroni (rectangular-shaped U). Many of the shanks of carving tools are bent to allow a scooping action (Fig.66).

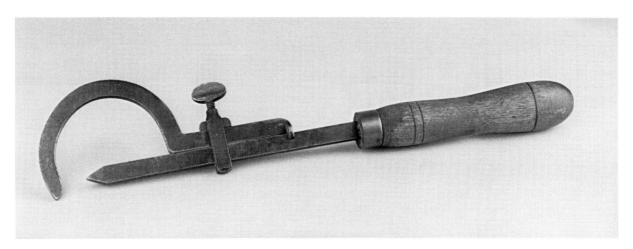

Fig. 65 Turner's sizing tool, sometimes called woodturner's gauge.

KNIVES

The knife needs little introduction to anyone. Man or woman, young or old, everyone knows what a knife is and almost anyone can use one. Knives as we know them, kitchen knives, penknives, and hunting knives, were not used much in woodworking, as there were more efficient tools for cutting and paring. There are, however, a few tools (some with the word knife in their titles) that were used in woodworking. There are other tools which are knife-like, such as slitters, but are not considered edge tools. They will be found in the chapter on Measuring Tools, under Gauges and Slitters.

DRAW KNIFE

The most common of the woodworking knives, drawknives can be found in most any flea market. There are two basic styles: flat and curved (Fig.67). The former was used for shaping the outside of barrel staves, roof shingles, ship masts, tool handles, and almost any other operation where large quantities of wood had to be removed freehand. The curved knives were used mostly by coopers for shaping the inside (or concave) part of the stave.

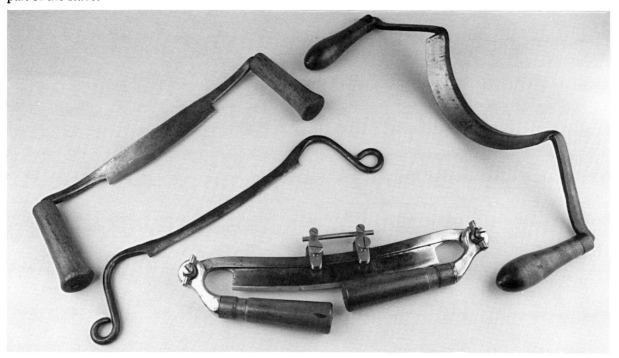

Fig. 67 *Various types of drawknives.*

SCORP

Scorps were nothing more than a form of a curved drawknife, generally used where more curvature was needed. They were open or closed, one-handed or two-handed (Fig.68). In some cases they were merely drawknives heated red hot and bent into a tighter curve. These makeshift scorps do not have the value of the true handforged ones. Another tool that is mistaken for a true scorp is the factory-made box scraper (Fig.69). Most tool authorities agree that the box scraper was used to scrape labels off wooden boxes and not to shape a concavity. It is considerably more shallow in curvature than a true scorp.

Fig. 68 *Scorps. The two on the left are closed; the one on the right, open.*

Fig. 69 *Box scraper.*

COOPER'S CHAMFER KNIFE

This was a true paring tool, although its shape doesn't fit the image of a knife (Fig.70). Once the top of the barrel was leveled, the chamfer knife, guiding off this level surface with its horizontal iron handle, was used to bevel or chamfer the inside edge. These knives were made right or left handed, based upon whether the cooper wanted to work clockwise or counter-clockwise. The blade edge varied from 3" to 6" wide.

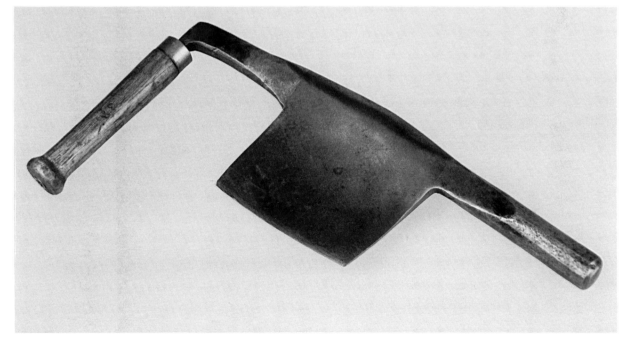

Fig. 70 *A cooper's chamfer knife.*

CABINETMAKER'S KNIFE

Most every cabinetmaker had a general purpose knife in his tool kit. Some were quite elaborate, with the blade removable for easy replacement and also to utilize different shaped tips. Often the handle was decorative, sometimes with ebony in a brass frame. Such knives can still be found in cabinetmaker's shops today (Fig.71).

Fig. 71   Cabinetmaker's knife.

BLOCK or BENCH KNIFE

This knife, which came in various shapes, was hooked into a bench ring and the work was pared by operating the long handle forged to the blade (Fig.72). They normally were 2' to 3' long, with some even longer ones (called clogger's knives) used for making wooden shoes.

Fig. 72   Block, or bench, knives.

RACE KNIFE

An interesting collectible, the race knife was used to scribe timber with the owner's identification marks, and to number pieces of framing lumber for ease of assembly. The scribing was done with the U-shaped knife blade which cut a groove or "race." Some knives have a pointed tip which acted as a compass leg for making curved marks or races. Sometimes these tips have been broken off, reducing the value of the tool. Fig.73 shows a handforged knife.

Fig. 73   Race knife.

FROE or RIVING KNIFE

A froe is not a knife. It doesn't cut; it splits, much as a wedge does. As such, it deliberately was never kept sharp. If you find a froe ground to a fine knife edge, it was done mistakenly. Froes were almost all handforged (although contemporary factory- made ones are sold to users today). They were used to split-out pieces of lumber that would be completely with-the-grain, for ease of bending and greater strength. It was also much faster to rive (split out) shingles or chair parts from a log than to cut each piece with a saw (Fig.74)

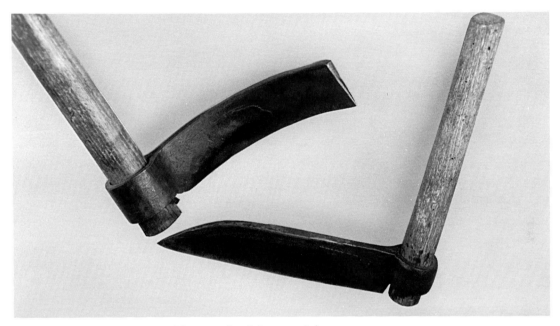

Fig. 74   On the left, a curved froe; on the right, a straight one.

BARK SPUD

A spud is also not a true knife, but it is close enough to be included in this category. The spud was used predominantly in the pulpwood and tanning industries. It forces the bark away from the wood by a prying action. Like a froe, it is not sharpened to a fine edge. This prevents the blade from digging into the wood; instead it slides between the wood and the bark. Some of the many types of spud tips are shown in Fig.75.

Fig.75   Bark spuds.

CROOKED KNIFE

This knife gets its name from the fact that the blade is bent at the handle to fit the cutting angle as it is drawn backwards (palm facing up) toward the user. It is used to carve handles and other similar shaped objects almost in a whittling fashion. It had its origins in New England, particularly in the state of Maine. More often than not, the blade is an old straight razor and is wrapped into the handle with copper wire, leather or string. The handle is also bent to accommodate the fingers in the closed fist position. Some of these knives are works of art, with elaborate carvings and inlays (Fig.76).

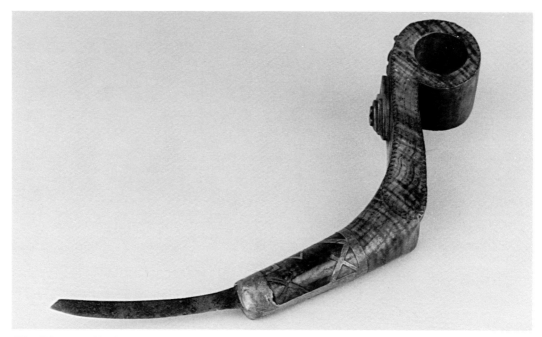

Fig. 76   *A highly decorated crooked knife dated 1897.*

PLANES

WOODEN PLANES

Wooden planes date back at least to Roman times and are often shown in medieval manuscripts, stained glass windows, and stone and wood carvings. By the 17th century western European woodworkers were carving dates along with decorative motifs on their planes, providing us with historic reference points. Surviving examples from this period are most often Dutch, German or Austrian and, if authentic, are much sought after (Fig.77).

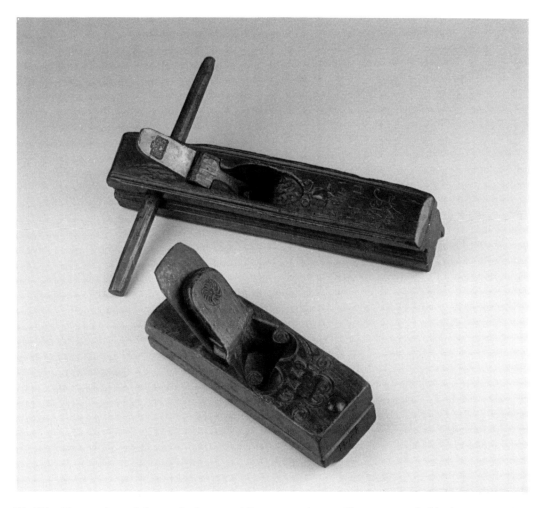

Fig.77 *Two early and decoratively carved European planes. The upper probably Austrian or German and dated 1787. The lower, Dutch, is dated 1770.*

Some time around the end of the 17th century planemaking became a recognized trade. Earlier, woodworkers had made their own planes, buying only the cutter blades (called irons) from a blacksmith or edge tool maker. These new professional planemakers had one characteristic different from most other toolmakers. They frequently imprinted their names, and sometimes the town or city where they worked, on the front (or toe) of the plane, rather like an artist signing his canvas. This tradition enables us to identify, locate, and date many of these planes (Fig.78).

Fig.78 *A few of the several thousand planemaker imprints. F. Nicholson (1683-1753) of Wrentham, Massachusetts, is generally believed to be the first American planemaker to imprint his name on his work. R.W. Hendrickson made planes and ran a tool shop in New York City in 1859. Israel White (1804-39) was a prominent Philadelphia planemaker. Barton & Smith operated in Rochester, NY, in 1842 and was one of several planemaking entities operated by David R. Barton.*

It also adds a dimension almost unique to wooden plane collecting. Not only can planes be collected by type of plane, but also by maker. To date almost 3000 American, Canadian, and English planemakers have been identified. Their biographical data and imprints now appear in readily available reference books (see Books to Read, page 193).

The first planes used in the U.S. were brought from England and the Continent by early immigrant artisans. These were primarily the simpler types, used to prepare and finish the wood surface and to join boards. The first recorded English planemaker was Thomas Granford who made planes in London, probably before 1700. One of his apprentices was Robert Wooding, who worked in London 1710-28. A number of Wooding planes have survived. Some of these have been found in the United States under circumstances indicating that they were brought here by early woodworkers.

The first recorded American planemaker, Francis Nicholson of Wrentham, Massachusetts, began his planemaking not long after Wooding, his working years being sometime between 1728 and 1753. But the English planes predominated, certainly in the seaport cities of Boston, New York, Philadelphia, and Baltimore, where mercantile connections, tradition, and the relative ease and economy of sea transportation favored the English makers. In addition to planes, plane irons were imported in large numbers from Sheffield and Birmingham.

The appearance of the first professional planemakers coincided with changes in architectural and furniture styles and the use of more ornamental moldings. To meet these changes, new types of planes evolved and molding profiles became more complex. The earliest colonial planemaking developed in the area between Boston and Providence, beginning in Wrentham, Massachusetts, and spreading outward: the Nicholsons, father and son, and Cesar Chelor, their freed slave, in Wrentham, Samuel Doggett in Dedham, Henry Wetherel in Norton, John Walton and his sons in Reading, all Massachusetts towns; and Jonathan Ballou and Jo. Fuller in Providence, Rhode Island.

The planes made by these early New Englanders differed from those of their countrymen to the south and of the English in several ways. They used yellow birch, rather than the beech used by the others. Their plow planes had a distinctive style and, not surprisingly, are called Yankee plows. The New Englanders also tended to lag the English and the colonies to the south in reducing the size of their molding planes to the final standard length of 9½". We find many of their early planes still measuring 9⅞" to 10" right up to and through the Revolutionary War.

By the 1760's planemakers also began to appear in the mid- Atlantic area: Thomas Grant and James Stiles in New York City, Samuel Caruthers and Benjamin Armitage in Philadelphia. But most planes were still imported from England until after the Revolution.

That war, and the economic distress that followed it, created a hiatus in the economy that lasted for almost a decade, until the adoption of the new constitution and the election of Washington as President. In the 1790s the new country recovered its prosperity and growth resumed. This too affected planemaking and, for the first time, Americans began to produce planes in quantity.

Important names of this period, 1790-1810, include: New Englanders Jo. Fuller and John Lindenberger of Providence, Rhode Island; Aaron Smith of Rehoboth, John Sleeper of Newburyport, Nicholas Taber of New Bedford, William Raymond of Beverly, Levi Little of Boston, all in Massachusetts; and Henry Wetherell of Chatham, Connecticut. John Stiles was active in Kingston, New York. In Philadelphia there was a large group of makers: Thomas Napier, William Brooks, Thomas Goldsmith, John Butler, Amos Wheaton, and William Martin, all producing planes in the English style.

Further to the west in Lancaster County, Pennsylvania, Dietrich Heiss and his son Jacob were active, and further south in Maryland, William Vance and John Keller began the tradition of the Baltimore makers.

During the early years of the 19th century, the country moved westward into the Ohio territories and beyond. Cincinnati became an important planemaking center, and later St. Louis. The number of planemakers proliferated. Their various business endeavors prospered and failed as the country was periodically racked with panics and war. By the second quarter of the 19th century, the wooden plane had reached its zenith. The introduction of machines, the use of water and steam power, and the great improvements in transportation and communication led to the formation of larger companies, the use of convict labor, and the development of distribution systems that reached far beyond the place where the planes were made. This period also saw the beginnings of the metal plane, which would soon supersede the wooden one. By the 1880s the end was in sight. Though wooden planes continued to be offered into the 20th century, it was to a shrinking market.

The concept of the plane is quite simple. Think of it as a chisel, which is what the plane iron really is, held in a rigid frame. Its purpose is to remove wood from a surface in order to shape it, fit, or finish it, or perhaps a combination of the three. The plane body holds and controls the chisel, or iron. It keeps it on course and, depending on how much of the iron is exposed, it controls the amount of wood being removed. What could otherwise be done only by a highly skilled craftsman at great cost in time and energy when using a hand chisel could now be accomplished quickly and efficiently by a reasonably proficient workman using a plane. No wonder R.A. Salaman in his *Dictionary of Tools* calls the invention of the plane "the most important advance in the history of woodworking tools in the last 2000 years."

BENCH PLANES

Bench planes are the oldest and most common form of planes. Called bench planes because they were most often found on the workbench, they come in four basic types, smooth, jack, fore plane, and jointer. All have a flat sole, an iron generally held at a 45° angle to the body, and no side throat opening, but instead, a wide mouth at the top of the plane for the escape of shavings (Fig.79 and Fig.80).

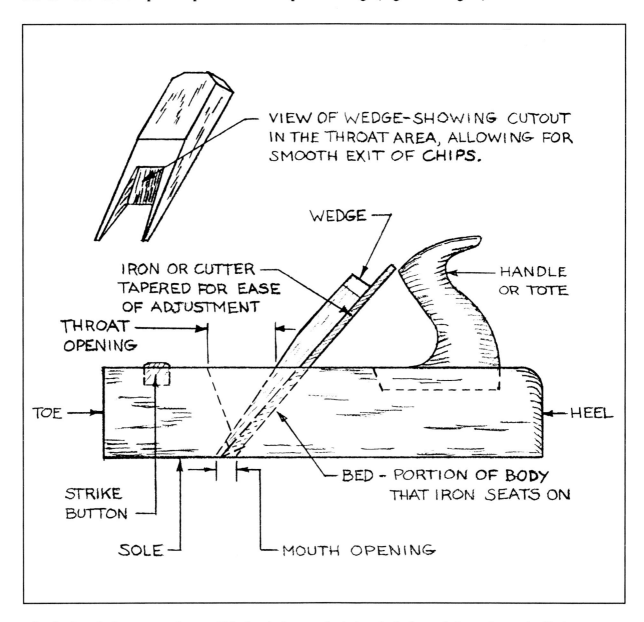

Fig.79 *Bench plane nomenclature. This sketch shows a single iron jack plane. In later planes, double irons were often used, with a top or cap iron screwed to the cutting iron to curl and break the chip. The plane bed was cut out to admit the cap screw. The strike buttons were not a decorative device, but served a functional purpose. When they were struck sharply with a mallet, they loosened the wedge and allowed the user to remove or adjust the plane iron (or cutter). Look at an old bench plane without a strike button and you will see evidence of dents and splintering at the position where the button would otherwise be.*

Fig.80 *The four major categories of bench planes. From the top: jointer, fore plane, jack, and smoother.*

SMOOTH PLANE

Most often 6½" to 10½" long and used to do the final finishing and smoothing on the surface of the wood. The longer versions (9" to 10½") usually have handles (Fig.80).

JACK PLANE

14" to 16" long and the most widely used of all the bench planes. It is used for planing off the most amount of wood in the least amount of time, i.e. for the rough, or preliminary work, with the finishing then done by the smooth plane or fore plane. It almost always has an open handle (Fig.80).

FORE PLANE

Usually 18" to 22" long with a closed handle. Less common than the jack plane, it is used to smooth off the work after using a jack; or it precedes the jointer, hence the name "fore" plane. However, in many cases, a fore plane was not owned at all and the workman went from the jack plane to the smoother or jointer. The English call the fore plane a try plane (Fig.80).

JOINTER PLANE

22" to 30" long and most often used to make the finishing passes on the long straight edges of the wood pieces preparatory to joining them. It has a closed handle (Fig.80).

OTHER FINISHING PLANES

MITER PLANE

Similar in appearance to the smooth plane except that the iron is set at a 35° (or lower) angle to the body rather than the 45° of the smoother. It is used to trim the end grain of wood and also for work on difficult-grained woods like birds-eye and burl. Since it can be held in one hand, it is also convenient for a wide variety of other finishing and fitting work (Fig.81).

TOOTHING PLANE

Much the same size and shape as the smoother, except that the iron is almost vertical to the body and is serrated. Used to ridge the wood prior to glueing veneer, or to level difficult grain (Fig.81)

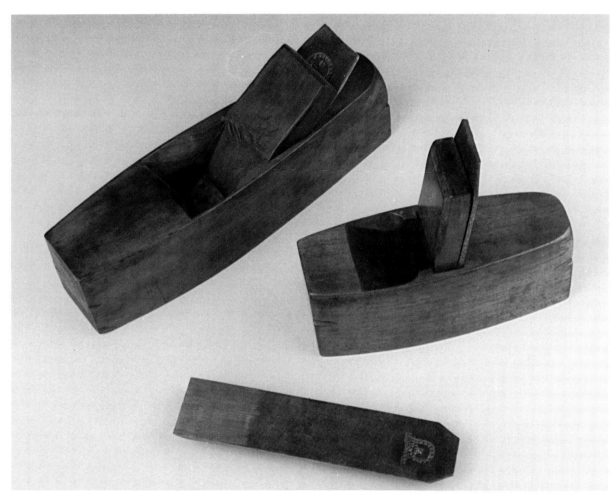

Fig.81 *Above, an American miter plane; below, a toothing plane and a toothing plane iron.*

CIRCULAR or COMPASS PLANE

Similar to the smoother in appearance and use, except that the sole is convex from front to back, enabling the plane to be used on curved surfaces. Some of these planes have an adjustable front drop that permits the user to vary the arc of the cut (Fig.82).

Fig.82   Circular or compass planes. The one on the left has an adjustable front drop.

MINIATURE PLANE

Sometimes as small as 2"—3", these planes were used predominantly by model makers and instrument makers for shaping and smoothing (Fig.83).

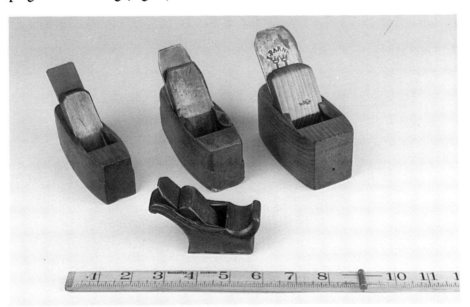

Fig.83   Miniature planes.

PLANES USED FOR CUTTING JOINTS

RABBET (also called a REBATE)

Used to cut away a step (called a rabbet) along the edge of the wood that will accommodate another piece of wood to make an overlapping joint. The plane is usually flatbottomed with the iron extending slightly beyond the full width of the sole. The edge of the iron is set square across the body for working with the grain, or skewed (diagonally across the body) for easier cutting, particularly on cross grain. The plane can optionally have one or two side-cutters (called nickers) in advance of the iron to score the wood to prevent chipping when working across the grain. A distinguishing feature of the rabbet is the gracefully curved open throat for shavings to escape (Figs.84 and 85).

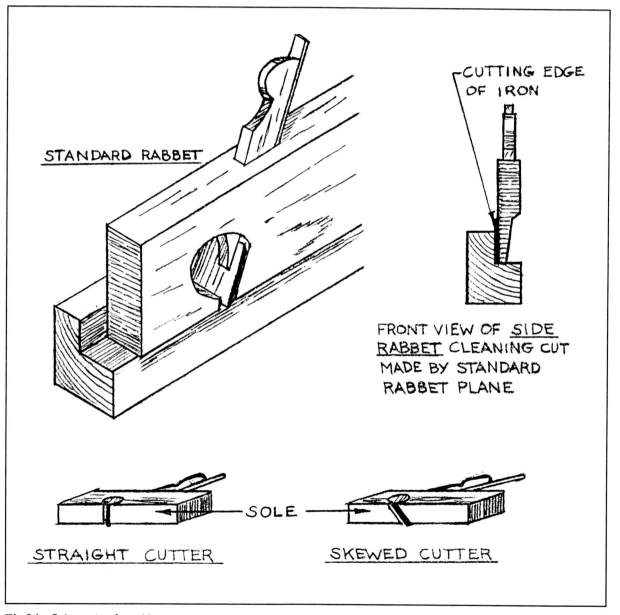

Fig.84 *Schematic of a rabbet.*

Fig.85   Several types of rabbet planes. Left, a common rabbet; center, an open handled ship's jack rabbet with two nickers; right, a closed handle skewed rabbet with one nicker.

SIDE RABBET

Has a cutting edge that extends up the side of the plane body rather than along the bottom, and the iron is almost perpendicular to the body. This plane is used to clean and widen the side of a rabbet cut and was sold in pairs for a right- and left-hand cut, so the user could always follow the grain of the wood (Fig.86).

Fig.86   A pair of side rabbets; right and left hand examples.

FILLETSTER (also called a FILLISTER)

Used for the same purpose as the rabbet, except that the filletster has a moveable fence that controls the width of the rabbet cut. In addition, it usually has a depth stop on the side opposite the fence to control the depth of the cut. The most common filletster (the moving filletster) has the fence attached directly to the sole of the plane and has a narrow throat opening like that of the sash filletster. The screw arm or wedge arm models have the wide curved throat opening of the rabbet plane and the fence attached to the arms (Fig.87).

Fig.87 *Filletsters: left ,a screw arm toted filletster; right, a moving filletster.*

SASH FILLETSTER
(also called SASH FILLISTER)

A specialized plane used to cut the rabbet in window sash. Most of these planes are English-made; American models are rare. Two types of fence arms were made, wedge arm and screw arm. Unlike that on the filletster above, the fence is set higher and it doesn't slide under the body of the plane but into the side. Also the depth stop is located on the same side of the plane as the fence. A sash filletster usually has a boxwood wear strip (called boxing) dovetailed into its sole and side. The boxwood, together with the brass fittings and delicate proportions, make it a particularly appealing plane (Fig.88).

Fig.88 *Sash filletster.*

SASH PLANE

For making window frames. It is made in two types: one employing a single iron consisting of two distinct sections; or (the more common) consisting of two separate irons, one cutting a rabbet and the other a molding. In this way both the shoulder for the glass and the decorative inside molding are cut at the same time. It is usually 9½"—10" long and unhandled. Some styles have solid bodies, while others are split lengthwise with adjusting screws and shims for spacing. The premier examples are adjusted with arms and locking nuts or wedges similar to plow planes. The construction of windows was one of the most interesting and demanding jobs of the housewright or joiner (Figs.89 and 90).

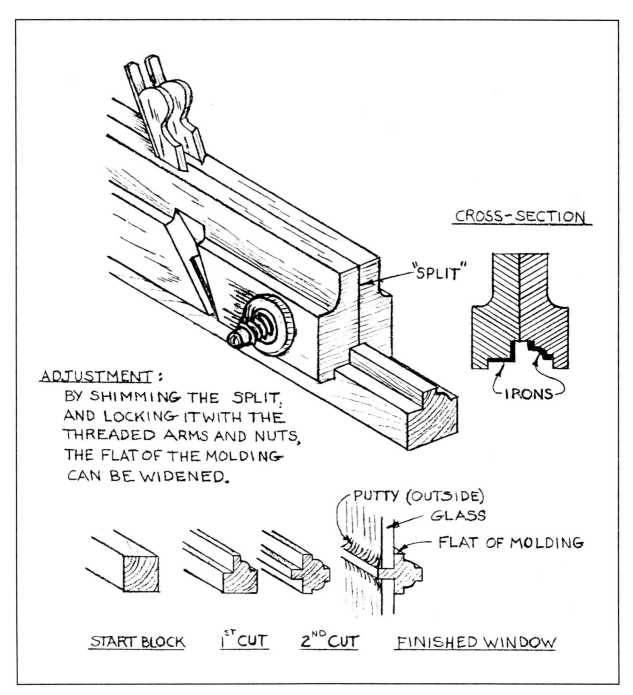

CROSS-SECTION

"SPLIT"

IRONS

ADJUSTMENT:
BY SHIMMING THE SPLIT,
AND LOCKING IT WITH THE
THREADED ARMS AND NUTS,
THE FLAT OF THE MOLDING
CAN BE WIDENED.

PUTTY (OUTSIDE)
GLASS
FLAT OF MOLDING

START BLOCK   1ST CUT   2ND CUT   FINISHED WINDOW

Fig.89 Schematic showing sash plane in use.

Fig.90 *Types of sash planes. From left to right: single iron/solid body, double iron solid body, double iron/split body with adjustable screws, and double iron/split body with adjustable screw arms.*

PLOW PLANE

Used to cut a groove, with the grain, parallel to the edge of the wood. The plow permits the user greater flexibility than was previously available in one plane (Fig.91). Sets of eight or more plane irons in varying widths, allows one plow plane to do the work of a whole range of rabbets or other grooving planes (Fig.92). The length of the fence arms, and the ability to adjust the fence, allows a wide choice as to how far from the edge of the wood the groove can be cut; and the adjustable depth stop lets the user easily control the depth of the groove.

The standard plow plane was made in three basic styles, the slide arms locked by wedges (Fig.93), the slide arms locked by thumbscrews (Fig.94), and the screw arms locked by nuts (Fig.95), referring to the ways in which the fence arms were locked to the body of the plane. A fourth type, the Yankee plow was developed and used in New England during the 18th and very early 19th centuries, after which it was superseded by the standard plow. The Yankee plow tended to be longer (usually 10"), the fence did not extend beyond the body, and the arms were square and mortised into the fence. The arms were almost always secured by thumbscrews, though occasionally with wedges.

Screw arm plow planes often have handles, wedge arms rarely, and Yankee plows never. Handled planes cost more; so did plows made of the more exotic woods such as boxwood, rosewood, and ebony. These made spectacular looking tools, especially when ivory was used for the locking nuts and tips of the arms. They often were presentation pieces or owned for show rather than use. The ultimate example was a "handled ivory plow plane with solid gold nuts and washers, 22 carats fine, golden tips on arms and golden mounted" offered by L. & C.H. DeForest in their 1860 price list for $1000, the price of a house in those days. No example has been reported to date.

Plow plane arms, no matter how they were secured, tended after time to work loose. In an attempt to maintain "parallellism," i.e., keep both arms and thereby the fence equidistant from the plane body, a number of interesting approaches were developed (Fig.96).

Continental European plow planes are often seen in the U.S. Unlike the English and American types, whose arms are attached to the fence and pass through holes in the plane body, the European plows have their fence arms attached to the body of the plane and pass through holes in the fence. There are other differences in size, type of wood used, and hardware, but the fixing of the arms is the surest clue (Fig.97).

A word of caution regarding the arms on screw arm plows. Move the locking nuts on the arms so that the threads on the arms can be examined. An occasional dink or chip in the threading is normal, but more pervasive damage is difficult to repair and greatly reduces the value of the piece.

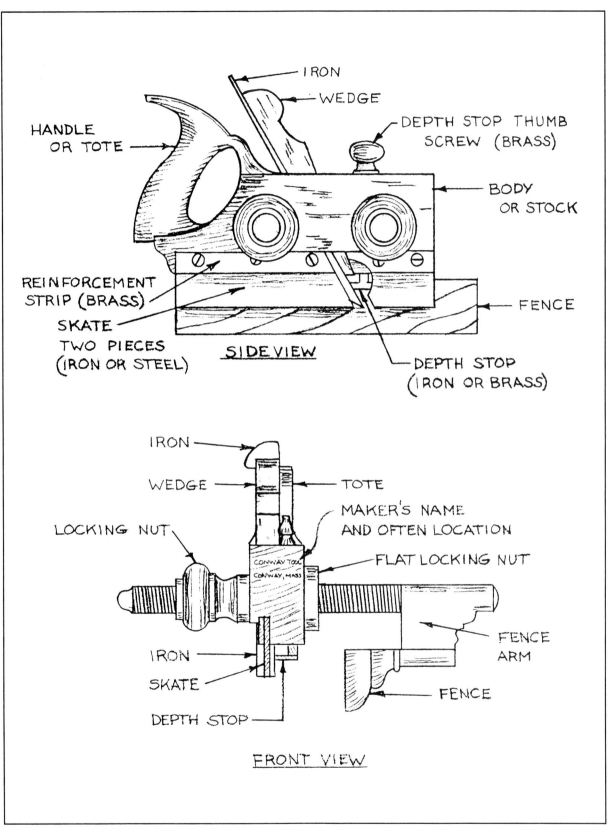

IRON

WEDGE

HANDLE
OR TOTE

DEPTH STOP THUMB
SCREW (BRASS)

BODY
OR STOCK

REINFORCEMENT
STRIP (BRASS)

SKATE
TWO PIECES
(IRON OR STEEL)

SIDE VIEW

FENCE

DEPTH STOP
(IRON OR BRASS)

IRON

WEDGE

TOTE

MAKER'S NAME
AND OFTEN LOCATION

LOCKING NUT

CONWAY TOOL
CONWAY, MASS

FLAT LOCKING NUT

FENCE
ARM

IRON

SKATE

DEPTH STOP

FENCE

FRONT VIEW

Fig.91 *Schematic of a screw arm plow plane circa 1850. The body, fence, and wedge are usually of the same wood. Most common is beech; fruitwood and boxwood are next, then rosewood, then ebony.*

Fig.92 *A set of eight plow plane irons.*

Fig.93 *Wedged arm plow plane.*

Fig.94 *Slide arm plow plane secured by thumbscrews.*

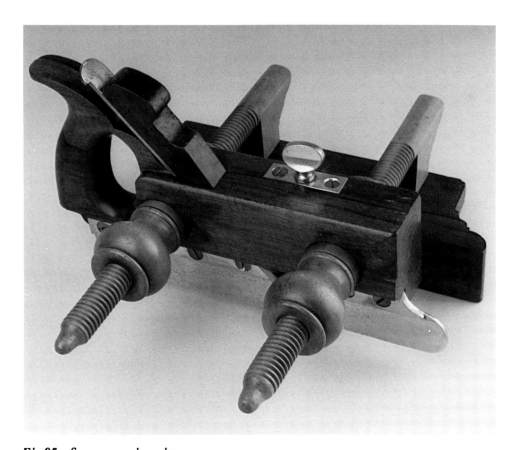

Fig.95 *Screw arm plow plane.*

Fig.96 *Two examples of the attempt to achieve parallelism of the plow plane's fence to its body. On the left an English bridle plow; on the right Israel White's 1834 patented three-arm plow plane.*

Fig.97 *Two continental European plow planes.*

DADO PLANE

The purpose of the dado is similar to that of the plow, but the dado is designed to cut a groove across the grain without tearing the wood. To accomplish this the iron is skewed so that only a portion of the blade first meets the wood, much as the prow of a ship cuts through water. The main iron is preceded by a vertical iron that severs the wood fibers on either side of the cut, preventing gouging. Additionally the dado has a depth stop (Fig.98).

Fig.98 Dado planes.

TONGUE and GROOVE or MATCH PLANES

A set of two matching planes, one of which cuts a tongue down the center of the edge of a board and the other of which cuts a corresponding groove in the board to be joined (Fig.99). Tongues and grooves sometimes were combined in one plane (Fig.100). They also came in sets with longer bodies (13"—14") and some with an adjustable fence similar to that of a plow plane. These longer planes were called match plank tongue and groove (Fig.101). Match planes usually have the size of the stock width that they cut stamped on their heels, normally from ¼" to ¾".

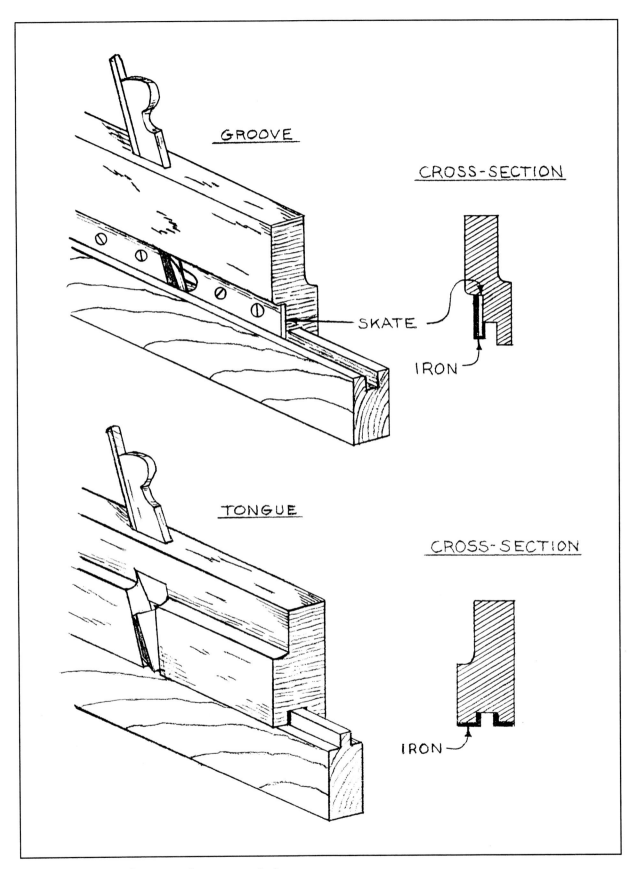

GROOVE

CROSS-SECTION

SKATE

IRON

TONGUE

CROSS-SECTION

IRON

Fig.99 *Schematic of tongue and groove match planes.*

Fig.100 *On the left, matched tongue and groove planes; on the right, a combined "coming and going" tongue and groove plane.*

Fig.101 *Match plank tongue and groove.*

PLANES USED FOR CUTTING DECORATIVE SHAPES

HOLLOW and ROUND PLANE

These most common molding planes were usually sold in nine different size pairs, although they were often available in 24 pairs. The hollow has a shallow concave iron, while the round has a shallow convex iron (Fig.102 and Fig.103). The actual arc in both planes is ⅙ of a circle.

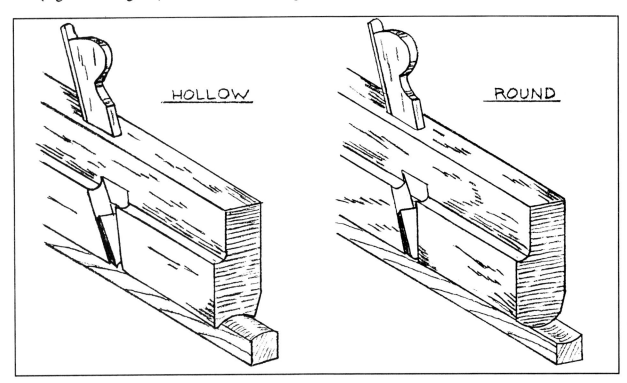

Fig.102   Schematic of hollow and round planes.

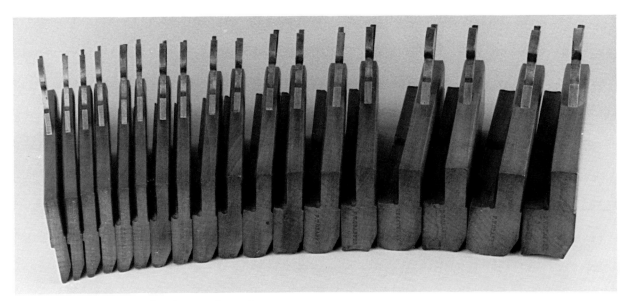

Fig.103   A matched set of hollows and rounds.

BEADING PLANE

A bead is a small, convex, half circle molding ending in a quirk (or narrow groove) on one or both sides. There are several kinds of beading planes, including the center bead which makes a bead in the center of the wood, and the side bead which makes a bead along the edge of the wood (Fig.104). Beads are among the most frequently "boxed" planes. The term comes from the use of boxwood, a smooth durable wood used to reinforce the point of wear on the plane's cutting profile. In the better made beads the entire profile was often made out of boxwood, which was then dovetailed into the sole of the plane.

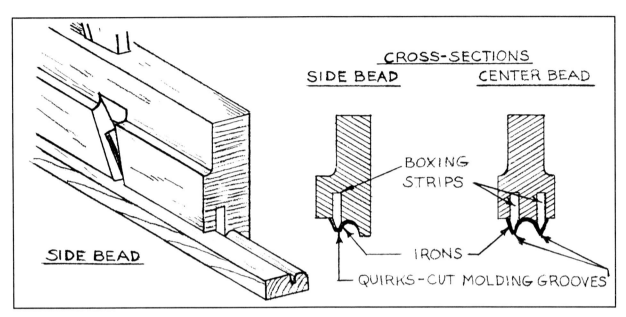

Fig.104   Schematic of a side bead.

ASTRAGAL PLANE

A form of bead with the half-circle starting and finishing on the same level, generally in fillets (flat sections) (Fig.105).

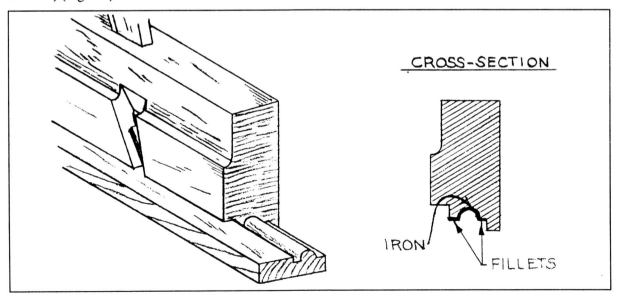

Fig.105   Schematic of an astragal.

OVOLO PLANE

A plane that cuts a convex molding, usually with fillets at each end. The Roman ovolo is a section of a circle (with the quarter round making a full quarter of a circle). The Grecian ovolo is a section of an ellipse, almost always ending in a quirk (Fig.106).

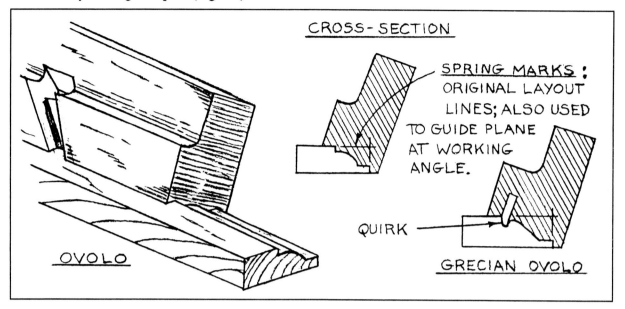

Fig.106 *Schematic of an ovolo.*

COVE PLANE

A plane that cuts a concave molding (deeper than that of the hollow plane). A cavetto is a section of a circle; a scotia a section of an ellipse. Unfortunately over the years the terms scotia, cove, and cavetto have been used interchangeably, creating much confusion (Fig.107).

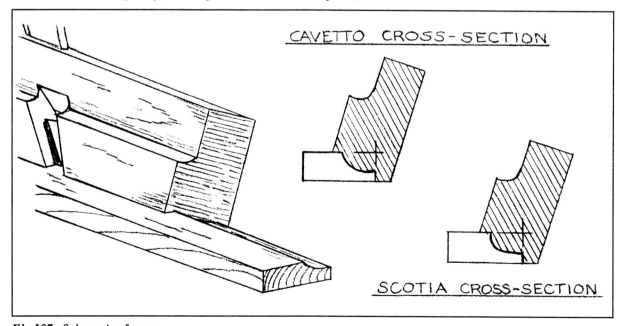

Fig.107 *Schematic of a cove.*

OGEE PLANE

A plane that cuts an S-shaped molding. A Roman ogee is a true "S" and a Grecian ogee is an elongated "S," almost always ending in a quirk. The profile can also be reversed (Fig.108).

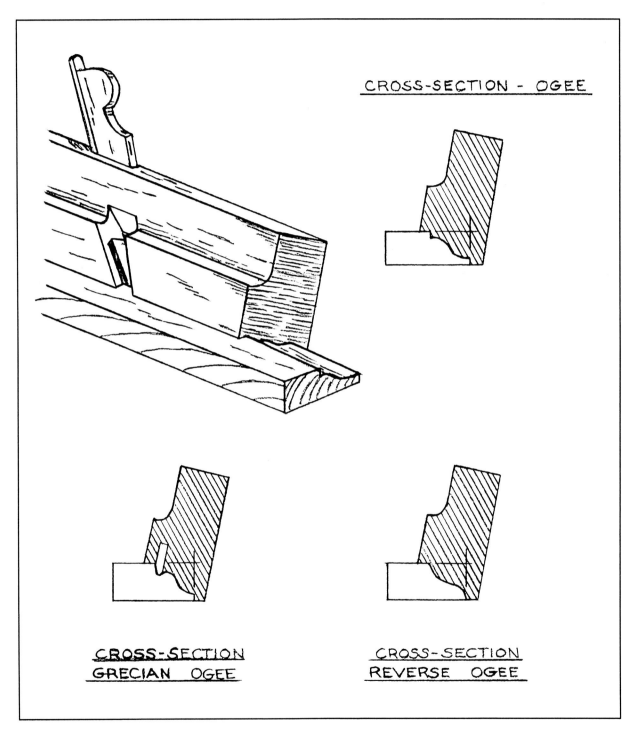

Fig.108   Schematic of ogees.

COMPLEX MOLDING PLANE

A plane composed of two or more of the simple moldings. Shown here are examples of molding profiles that were frequently used as architectural moldings. These are just three of the hundreds of varieties created to decorate everything from buildings and carriages to furniture and picture frames in the period before machine-made standardized molding became common (Fig.109). An interesting variation was the multiple iron complex molding plane (Fig.110). Those with three or four irons are usually Scottish.

The recutting of plane soles to change the plane's profile was a common practice of frugal woodworkers. It is often seen on molding planes. While it may have worked for the woodworker, it lowers the value of the plane for the collector. By reducing the height of the plane's body, it changes the plane's normal proportions, giving a clue to what has happened. Other clues: an enlarged plane mouth and boxing that now appears to be inlaid and serves little purpose. Other types of planes also are often altered. Many compassed smoothing planes are, in fact, converted regular smoothers, and gutter planes are often modified jack planes.

While on the subject of alteration, an improper wedge is not the same as a replaced wedge. An old plane that has had lots of use may not have its original wedge (or its original iron for that matter). A proper replacement is acceptable, although it reduces the value somewhat. However a wedge that is not of the same style as that of the maker, that doesn't fit properly or match the wood or patina of the plane body is not acceptable.

Fig.109   Three complex molding planes.

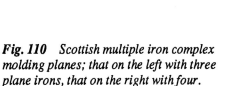

Fig. 110   Scottish multiple iron complex molding planes; that on the left with three plane irons, that on the right with four.

CORNICE PLANE or CROWN MOLDER

A wide plane cutting a large complex molding. Planes with irons under 3" in width are more apt to be called "cornice" and those with irons 3" or wider "crown." The plane is often equipped with front handles or a hole that can hold a rope, allowing the plane to be pulled by an assistant while the craftsman pushed from the rear using the handle (Fig.111). Because of the large amount of wood that had to be removed in making a crown molding, starter planes, resembling large hollows and rounds, were used to rough out the profile prior to finishing with the crown molder itself. The plane was called a crown molder by some since it was used to cut the moldings that trim the crown of a room, where the walls met the ceiling. The king of the molding planes, it is much prized by collectors, and priced accordingly. The largest known plane of this type is in the collection of the North Andover, Massachusetts, Historical Society. Made by William Raymond, of Beverly, MA, circa 1800, its cutting iron is 7¾" wide. Though supposedly made for use in the finishing construction of an Andover church, no examples of its molding profile have yet been found.

This is probably the appropriate place to warn about problems arising from worm holes and dry rot that are sometimes found in all types of planes but most often in the cornices and crown molders. Worm holes and dry rot can be real problems. Most worm holes are old and uninhabited, but occasionally they're not. Instead, the post hole beetle is happily at home and soon little piles of sawdust will appear. Be sure all the creatures are extinct, and check that the worm holes and burrowing have not done structural damage within. Dry rot is an even more serious problem. It will leave soft spots and the plane will not seem to be as heavy as it should be. Unless a plane is extremely rare or unique, don't get involved.

Fig.111 *An early crown molding plane.*

PLANES USED FOR CUTTING FUNCTIONAL SHAPES

RAISING PLANE or PANEL RAISER

Used to thin out a sloping area around the edges of a panel (as in door panels) so that the center of the panel stands out in relief and the edges are narrow enough to fit into the side grooves (Fig.112). Usually about 14" to 16" long and 2" to 4" wide, with a skewed iron. Most early examples have small integral fences (Fig.113). Later models tend to be wide and have adjustable fences (Fig.114).

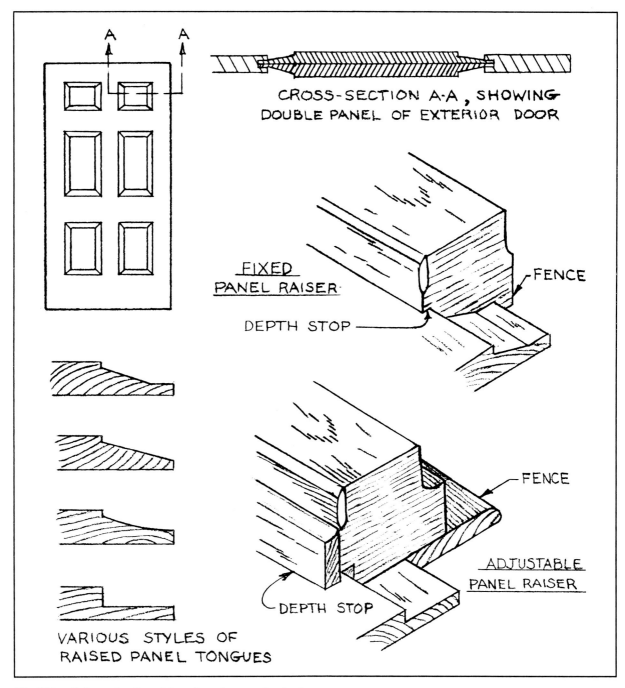

Fig.112 *Schematic of a raising plane (or panel raiser).*

Fig.113   *Two 18th century American panel raisers, both with integral fences.*

Fig.114   *19th century American panel raisers with adjustable fences.*

GUTTER PLANE or CONVEX JACK

A round-bottomed plane often modified from a flat-soled jack. The gutter plane was used to hollow out sections of wood to make building gutters. The shallower planes were also used for roughing out large crown moldings and other shapes (Fig.115).

Fig.115   *Gutter plane.*

PUMP LOG PLANE (also called PUMP PLANE)

Used to cut half sections that, when joined, became a wooden pipe (Fig.116).

Fig.116   *Pump log plane.*

CHAMFER PLANE

A plane used to remove the sharp corner or edge of a board by forming a bevel, usually at 45°. There are a number of different styles of chamfer planes, including some patented varieties (Fig.117).

Fig.117   Chamfer planes.

NOSING PLANE

For making the rounded front edge of a stair tread. The cutting edge of the iron is in the shape of a semi-circle. It can also be found with two irons, each making a half of the cut (Fig.118).

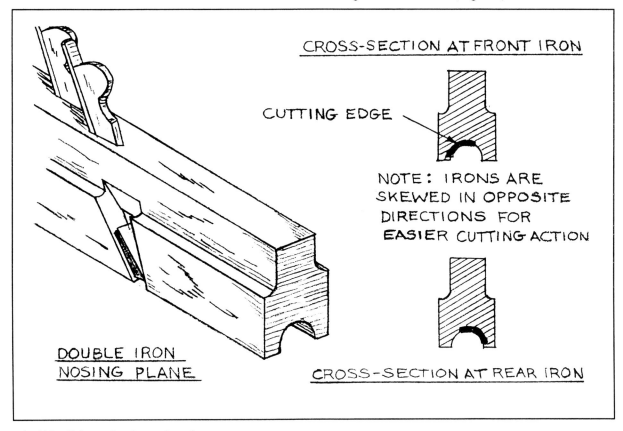

Fig.118   Schematic of a nosing plane.

SPECIALIZED PLANES

COOPER'S JOINTER

The longest jointers were used by coopers. These were between 3' and 6' long. They had no handles, but were kept in an upside down stationary position and the work run over the sole of the plane (Figs.119 and 121).

HOWEL, CROZE, and SUN PLANE.

These were planes used by the cooper in barrel making. The howel cut a shallow groove around the inside of the barrel, a few inches in from each end. The croze then cut a sharp groove in this surface to receive the top and bottom of the barrel. Both tools were rounded to fit the inside curvature of the barrel. The sun plane, or leveling plane, was used to even off the ends of the staves after they were assembled as a barrel. Again, the curvature of the plane reflected its use in working a round barrel (Figs.119, 120, and 121).

Fig.119 *Cooper's jointer and sun planes.*

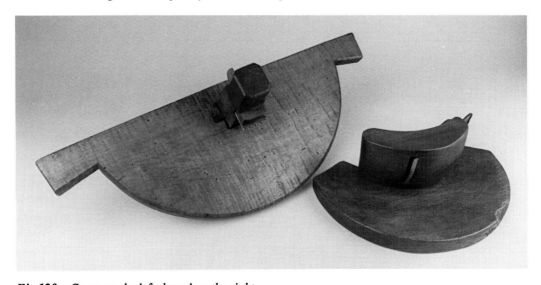

Fig.120 *Croze on the left; howel on the right.*

FINAL TRUEING OF STAVE ON THE COOPER'S LONG JOINTER

LEVELING WITH THE SUN PLANE

GROOVE CUT BY HOWEL

TO ASSEMBLE HEAD: HOOPS ARE LOOSENED AND HEAD IS FIT INTO CROZE GROOVE.

GROOVE CUT BY CROZE

Fig.121 *Some cooper's tools and how they're used. The cooper's jointer, sun plane, howel and croze.*

ROUTER

One style, called a "granny's tooth" or "old woman's tooth," was used to help cut a groove or to clean out the bottom of a groove. It was often craftsman-made and, as such, is found in a variety of styles, some having great aesthetic appeal (Fig.122).

Fig.122   Routers (sometimes called "granny's tooth").

COACHMAKER'S ROUTER

The coachmaker's routers were used to cut moldings, or grooves, in the curved sections of the coach. Some were unfenced, others fenced. To facilitate cutting "with the grain" at all times, some routers had two blades on opposite sides of the fence; others were made in pairs to achieve the same effect (Fig.123).

Fig.123   Top, two coachmaker's single routers; below, a coachmaker's double router.

COACHMAKER'S PLOW

Used for very much the same work as the coachmaker's router, but much rarer. It was able to plow out circular grooves in awkward areas (Fig.124).

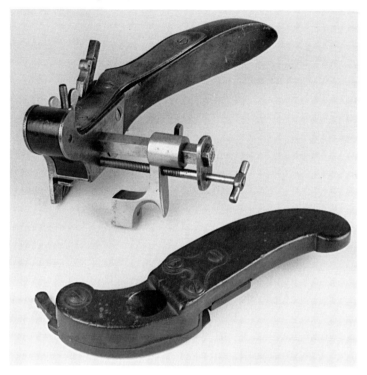

Fig.124   Coachmaker's plows. Above, a coachmaker's plow with an adjustable fence; below, fixed, also called French coachmaker's router.

COACHMAKER'S T-RABBET

A coachmaker's rabbet in which the sole of the plane is wider than its stock, leaving room for the craftsman's fingers when operating in a corner or in the confined spaces this type of work entailed (Fig.125). They were usually around 6" long, but sometimes miniaturized. T-rabbets were also made with convex soles (front to rear) to deal with the frequently encountered curved surfaces.

Fig.125   Coachmaker's T-rabbets, flat and convex.

COACHMAKER'S MOLDING PLANE

Fig.126 shows some examples of the many interesting coachmaker's planes used for the grooves and moldings that decorated coaches, carriages, and even early motor cars.

Fig.126   Coachmaker's molding planes.

SPILL PLANE

Not properly a plane in the woodworking sense, the spill plane creates tightly curled spiral shavings, called spills, which were used to take a flame from the fire to light a pipe, a candle, or perhaps, a lamp. A long distance, indeed, from flicking a light switch or a cigarette lighter. Spill planes were factory-made in the late 19th century, particularly in England, but most examples found are craftsman-made and come in a delightful variety of sizes and shapes (Fig.127).

Fig.127   Spill plane

ROUNDING PLANE

Sometimes called "witchets" they were used to round wood for such things as tool handles, dowels, ladder rungs, and spokes. The piece of wood to be rounded was held stationary, perhaps in a vise, and the rounding plane, starting at one end, was turned hand over hand down the length of the work (Fig.128).

Fig.128 *Rounding planes (or witchets). Left is fixed; right is adjustable.*

SHAVE

We might have categorized shaves under edge tools, particularly as they are sometimes, incorrectly we believe, combined with drawknives. However, we make the following distinction: edge tools have an entirely open blade, i.e. without a sole, without a mouth, and without a wedge, tang or screw to hold the blade. Edge tools do not have a variable depth of cut controlled by the blade extension from the sole. But that characteristic is the very essence of the plane. So we have elected to include shaves under planes, as they have soles, blade wedges or screws and a controlled depth of cut.

Shaves have their handles extending in a straight line to each other, directly out each side of the body (except a few curved shaves). In some cases the sole has an iron plate. Shaves "skim-cut," not scrape, and are generally small in size, with an approximately 2" — 4" long blade (Fig.130). They are most often used for smoothing wheel spokes, chair rungs, tool handles, and other rounded surfaces. Those shaves used for coopering, e.g. the downright, plucker, heading swift, straight shave, and inshave, are all considerably larger and heavier — in some cases over 12" across (Figs.129, 131 and 132). Other heavy shaves are the jarvis and nelson, used by the wheelwright, and the handrail shave (Fig.133).

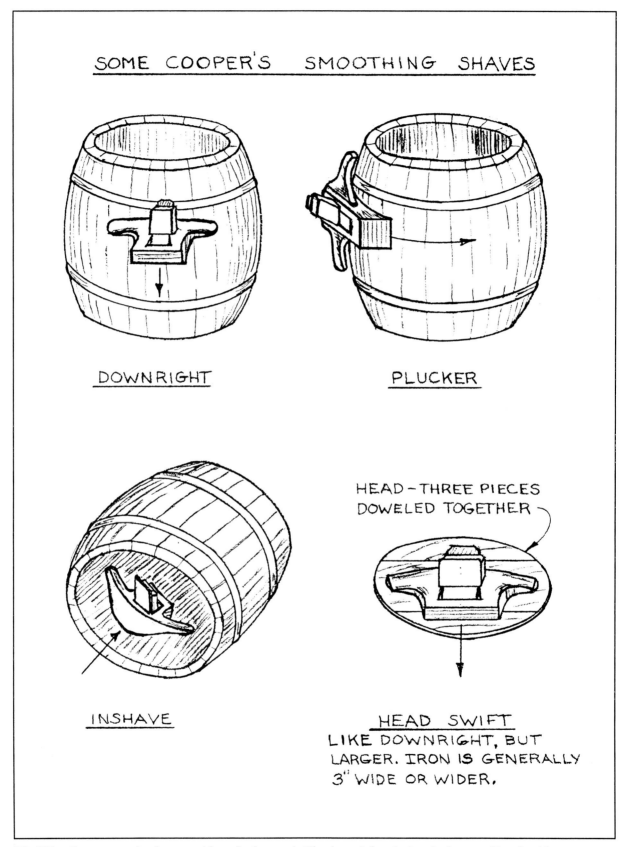

SOME COOPER'S SMOOTHING SHAVES

DOWNRIGHT

PLUCKER

INSHAVE

HEAD-THREE PIECES
DOWELED TOGETHER

HEAD SWIFT
LIKE DOWNRIGHT, BUT
LARGER. IRON IS GENERALLY
3" WIDE OR WIDER.

Fig.129   Some cooper's shaves and how they're used. The downright, plucker, inshave and head swift.

Fig.130 Hand shaves.

Fig.131 On the left, an inshave; on the right, a plucker.

Fig.132   *On the left, a head swift; on the right, a downright.*

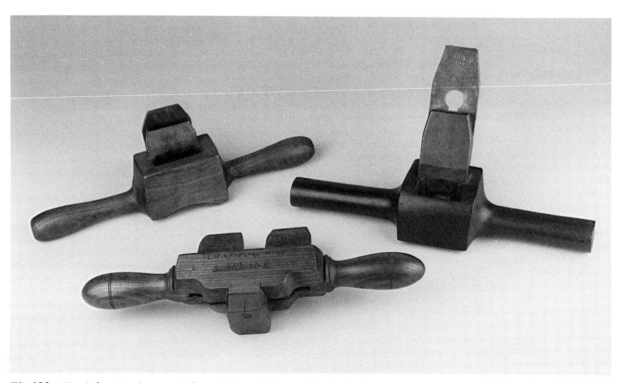

Fig.133   *Top left, a jarvis; top right, a Nelson; below, a handrail shave.*

BEADER

Beaders look very much like coach routers. The obvious difference is that they cut a bead or series of beads. One patented model, the Windsor beader (Fig.134), which scrapes rather than cuts, has a series of different-sized bead shapes on a single rotating wheel. The bodies of most, if not all, Windsor beaders are made of ebonized wood, not ebony.

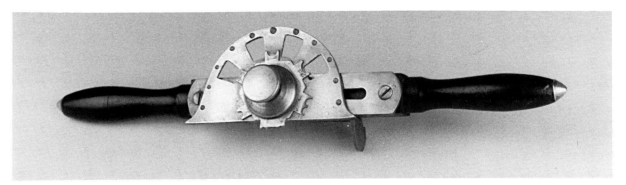

Fig.134   Windsor beader.

CONTINENTAL EUROPEAN PLANES

HORNED or BISMARCK PLANE

Most often found in the length of smoothing planes, these are usually of German or Austrian origin. Fig.135 shows an early chip-carved example and a later manufactured type.

Fig.135   Horned or Bismarck plane. The one below was chip carved by its owner.

FRENCH PLANE

Often quite decorative and sometimes made of cormier (servicewood), looking very much like our fruitwoods (Fig.136).

Fig.136   French planes.

DUTCH PLANE

Dutch planes were brought here, in many cases, by early settlers, and in later years by collectors. Fig.137 shows characteristic 19th century Dutch molding planes.

Fig.137   Dutch planes.

*Fig.138   Asiatic planes. Above, a carved Indonesian jack plane; below, a
Chinese smoothing plane. Chinese and Japanese planes are pulled toward the
user rather than pushed, as are European and American planes.*

We've only been able to provide basic information on the more frequently used planes. Readers who are interested in learning more about both these and the great number of the more specialized types are urged to refer to the Books to Read chapter.

DETERMINING AGE AND LOCATION OF A WOODEN PLANE

No matter what you are collecting, insight and judgment come with experience. There are no short cuts. One must read the literature, question and listen to more experienced collectors and look at and handle as many examples as possible. There are some basic rules however that can be very helpful in estimating the age and location of a plane. But please remember that when we generalize there will always be exceptions.

To begin with, you should always look first at the upper front end (the toe) of the plane to see if there's a maker's mark stamped into this area which is called the maker's slot. This is where the planemaker's imprint will appear; partly because of tradition, partly because the end grain took and held the imprint best. So if there's a maker's imprint you need only to look it up in a standard reference (see Books to Read) and you're likely to find a good deal of information including age and location. If there is no maker imprint then consider the following:

1. How long is the plane? American molding planes went to a standard 9½" length during the second quarter of the 19th century. Generally the longer the plane, the earlier it is. Planes 9⅞" — 10" long probably date before the American Revolution; 9⅝" — 9¾" indicates the last quarter of the 18th century to the early 19th century. Planes are sometimes found less than 9½" long, usually between 9¼" — 9⅜". These usually date from around 1800.

2. What kind of chamfering does the plane have along its top, and down the sides of its toe and heel? Wide flat chamfers (⅜" — ½") usually appear on planes made before 1800. Narrower flat chamfers (³⁄₁₆" — ¼") indicate circa 1800. Wide rounded chamfers (¼" — ⅜") usually appear on planes made between 1800 and 1830. After that, narrow rounded chamfers (⅛" — ¼") or no chamfers became the standard.

3. What kind of wood was used? Yellow birch usually means a plane made before 1800. Beech was used both early and late. Ebony, boxwood, rosewood, and lignum vitae usually indicate a date well after 1800.

4. On plow planes, riveted skates are early, usually before 1800; screwed skates after 1800. Slide arms secured by thumbscrews were used on the very early plows and continued to be used until around 1820. Screw arms appeared after 1800, most frequently after 1820-30.

5. The number of plane owners' marks on a plane can sometimes be helpful. Owners often marked their planes with their initials or names to identify their property. There are very old planes that have no owners' marks, but generally speaking, a plane with three or more different owners' marks will have been made before 1800.

6. Certain molding profiles were used during different architectural periods and can be used to help date the plane. Reference books are usually required for research in this area.

7. As the planemaker often imprinted his name in the maker's slot, so did he sometimes imprint his location.

8. The style of the wedge in the case of pre-mass-produced planes can often be a clue to location. Early wedges were highly individualized, reflecting the maker's aesthetic taste and the training he had received. Differences between wedges are sometimes quite subtle, but after a little practice you will begin to see them. Fig.139 shows some of the different styles. The Jo. Fuller wedge is relieved (cut away) in the back behind the finial. The relieved wedge is typical of late 18th century southeastern Massachusetts. The Sleeper wedge originated by John Sleeper (1754-1834) of Newburyport, MA, was subsequently adopted by other planemakers in that area. The E.W. Carpenter wedge is also distinctive. He worked in Lancaster, PA, ca.1820-60. Other nearby planemakers subsequently adopted a similar wedge style. Francis Nicholson, the first documented American planemaker, who worked before the American Revolution, used a wedge outline sometimes called the "Wrentham" type wedge (named after his hometown of Wrentham, MA). This style was adopted by some of his contemporaries in that area.

9. Boxing was used in molding planes to reinforce points of wear in the cutting profile. Usually boxwood was used (thus the term boxing), but in Philadelphia and sometimes in Boston and Baltimore lignum vitae was often substituted.

10. Exotic woods such as ebony and lignum came into the United States from the tropics, often as ships' ballast (they are heavier than water). They were sometimes used to make bench planes, almost always by planemakers located in the seaport areas. The handled planes were often razeed, a style in which the portion of the plane's body where the handle sat was lower than the front. It was believed that the plane operated better because of a lower center of force. Razeed planes made of beech were also available from some of the larger commercial planemakers (Fig.140).

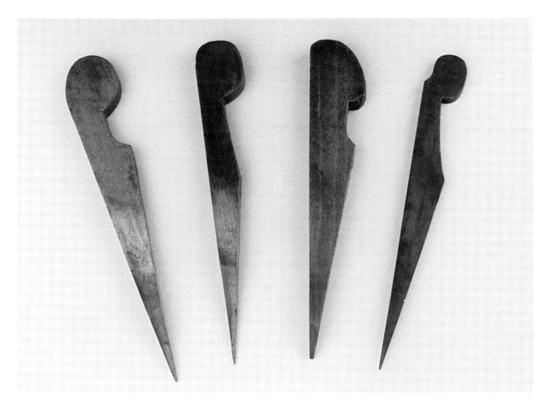

Fig.139   *Wedge styles. Left to right: Sleeper, Nicholson, Carpenter, Fuller (relieved).*

Fig.140   *Razeed bench planes.*

TRANSITIONAL or WOOD-BOTTOMED PLANES

The terms "transitional" and "wood-bottomed" are generally used interchangeably to describe that group of planes that started appearing around 1860 with wooden soles and iron blade-setting mechanisms, often set in iron upper bodies. The word transitional might give the impression that these planes bridged a gap of time between the all-wood and the all-metal planes. Time was not the bridging factor, as wood-bottomed and iron-bottomed planes arrived on the scene almost simultaneously. More likely, higher prices and the difference in "feel" were the reasons that all-metal planes did not enjoy full acceptance, although the iron setting-mechanisms common to both types did. To many woodworkers the wood-bottomed planes were the best of all worlds: they had more accurate blade-setting mechanisms than the all-wood planes, they had nice wooden soles that "wore-in," and they were cheaper than all-metal planes. There must be something to these points, since wooden planes with iron blade-setting mechanisms are still being manufactured today.

The Stanley Company entered the hand plane market in 1869 and provided the biggest impetus to the growth of American style planes. It did the most to develop model numbers and catalogs. By 1900 it dominated the field and today its name is still synonymous with hand tools and hardware.

Many plane patents have been issued since the first transitional emerged in the 1850's, but the basic shape and concept of the wood-bottomed plane have remained close to the originals. Shown in Fig.141 are two of the most common transitional shapes, the Stanley No. 24 smoother and the No. 27 jack. Almost all models, from Stanley and other manufacturers, looked like one of these, varying only in length and blade adjustment. Some of the other names that you may find on transitional planes are: Bailey, B-Plane (Birmingham), Chaplin, Gage (Fig.142), Keen Kutter, Ohio, Sargent, Siegley, Standard Rule, Union, and Winchester. Of all these names, only Stanley has survived and even it no longer makes wood bottomed planes.

Fig.141 Two transitional planes. At the top a Stanley No. 27 jack; below a No. 24 smoother.

Fig. 142   A Gage Tool Co. transitional smooth plane.

AMERICAN METAL PLANES

Interestingly, metal planes date back nearly as far as wooden ones. Planes with iron soles, rivets, and side plates (only the metal parts remain) have been found in what are now France, England and Germany, dating back to the second or third century A.D., when they were Roman provinces. Metal planes appear in medieval manuscripts, and there is an attractive iron block plane ca.1570 in the Dresden Historical Museum. So metal planes have been with us for some time. The modern metal plane was different however in that it used steel, was mass produced, widely distributed, and low in cost (Fig.143).

The metal plane, starting with early patented examples such as the Knowles bench planes of the 1820's (Fig.144), Holly's patent of 1852, and the Bailey patents of the 1850's, quickly grew to pre-eminence after the Civil War. Its accuracy and ease of use overcame whatever cost advantage the wooden plane had. By the 1870's the wooden plane was in retreat.

All planes, even the "completely wooden" ones, have some metal in them (at the least the cutting blade). To qualify as a metallic plane, the body and sole of the plane must be metal. The knob, handle, wedge, body insert (or fill), and even part of the sole, can be wood. The predominant metal used to cast these planes was iron, although on rare occasions gunmetal (bronze) was used. Stanley used gunmetal for two of its most prestigious, premium priced models, the No. 42 and No. 44 combination planes listed as the Millers Patents.

Brass was used by patternmakers to cast planes used in their trade, and sometimes to duplicate existing factory-made bench planes. Such examples should not be confused with bona fide factory-made planes. The recast planes are usually rougher in appearance and slightly shorter. Stanley also made six models from aluminum. Some of these are quite rare and are sometimes mistaken for their more common iron counterparts, even though they carry the prefix "A" before their style numbers.

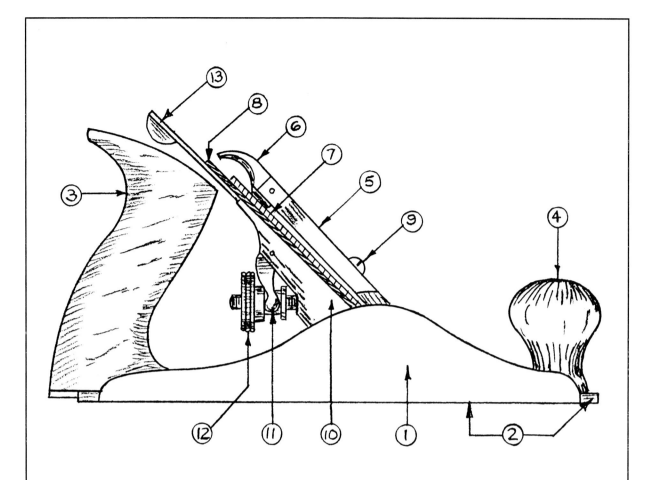

1. Body casting
2. Sole - integral part of the casting
3. Handle or tote - screws to sole; usually rosewood
4. Knob - screws to sole; usually rosewood
5. Cap - tightens irons by cam action of the toggle lever
6. Toggle lever - part of cap; pivots on pin through cap
7. Cap iron or top iron - screws to cutter; breaks chips
8. Cutting iron or cutter
9. Cap screw - screws into frog; holds cap and irons
10. Frog - screws into body; provides a bed for the irons
11. "Y" lever - extends into slot in cutter; pivots on pin through frog
12. Adjusting nut - screws in and out on stud; moves "Y" lever so as to adjust cutter for depth
13. Lateral adjustment lever - fits into cutter; aligns it laterally so as to have the cutting edge parallel to the mouth opening in the sole

Fig.143   A schematic of a metal smoothing plane. As simple as the nomenclature and the parts of the wooden planes are, the metal planes are exactly the opposite. This schematic shows a generic layout of the mechanics of a metal plane. For clarity, some parts have been simplified, and a few minor ones omitted. The parts we show are generalized. Designs varied among manufacturers and even among different models of the same manufacturer. Many of the Stanley planes were modified and improved over the years, and these changes can be used to help date the particular model. Even subtle differences in the knob or handle can indicate a model year.

Fig.144 *Above, the Knowles smoother. Patented in 1827, it is the earliest American patented metal plane. Below, a Birmingham Plane Co. rabbet patented in 1884.*

We will try to cover briefly the various types of metal planes that were most often used and therefore are most often found today. We will be referring primarily to planes made by the Stanley Tool Co., since Stanley had the most complete product line and manufactured these planes over the longest period and in the greatest quantities. Further, its products are documented in a series of catalogs spanning more than a century. Many of these catalogs have been reproduced and are currently available (see Books to Read p.193). In addition, metal planes bearing other trade names were actually produced by Stanley, e.g., Winchester and Keen Kutter.

The Stanley Company's expertise in management and marketing was a prime example of American industrial progress from the late 19th century to World War II. Stanley promoted growth in two important ways: it bought out its competition and it constantly introduced new models. Its aggressiveness in these areas was extraordinary and was responsible for the great number of models (over 300) that are available to plane collectors today.

Stanley persistently put something new in front of the buyer, whether he needed it or not. Many were improvements, but we suspect that there was a good percentage of new models that were more intriguing than useful. These planes are the rarest of all; they were either discarded by their new owners as "not worth the bother" or abandoned by Stanley for not selling well enough. Some examples that command high prices today are: No.42 gunmetal Miller's patent plow (Fig.145), No.A45 aluminum combination plow, No.56 core box, No.64 butcher block, No.87 scraper, No.101½ block, No.164 low angle, No.196 curve rabbet, No.212 scraper (Fig.146), No.340 furring, and No.444 dovetail. The average production life of these 11 planes was approximately 15 years, as opposed to the 60—70 years of most Stanley planes. The most notable example of the price/short-life correlation is the Millers 1872 patent plow (Fig.147). It was manufactured by Stanley for less than a year, not even long enough to warrant a model number. But this plane is now one of the most highly valued of all Stanley planes.

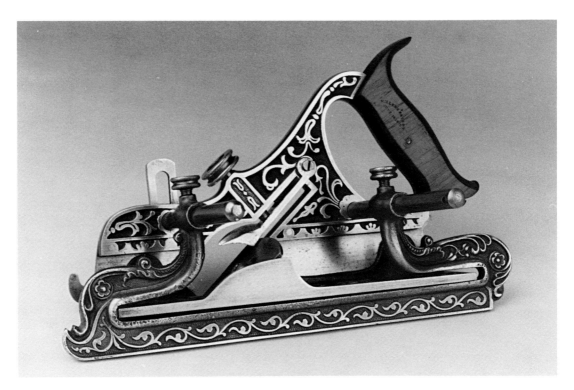

Fig.145   *The gunmetal Millers patent plow, Stanley No. 42.*

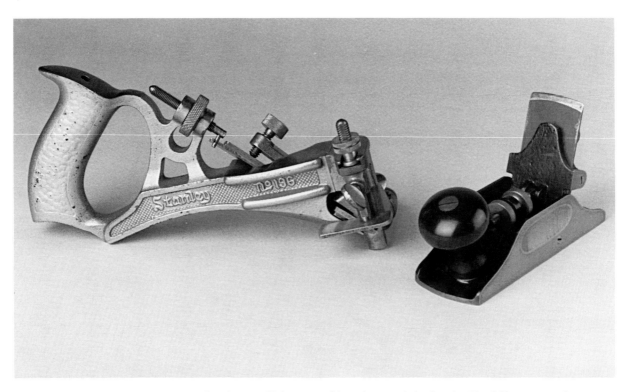

Fig.146   *Two Stanley classics: the Stanley No. 196 curve rabbet plane and the Stanley No. 212 scraper plane.*

Fig.147 *The Millers 1872 patent plow.*

Fig.148 *The Stanley Rule & Level Co. factory at New Britain, Conn.., ca.1872.*

BENCH PLANE

As was the case with wooden planes, this too is the commonest category of metallic planes. It ranges in size from the exalted Stanley No.1 at 5½" to the No.8 at 24" (Fig.149).

There was a wide variety of patented mechanisms, many of which concerned improvements in the adjustment of the cutting iron. Another interesting improvement was the use of a corrugated sole that helped to reduce friction between the sole of the plane and the wood being planed. These corrugated soles are rarest in the smaller sized planes (Nos.2 and 3), since such planes really didn't need the friction reduction.

Fig. 149 *Some Stanley bench planes. From the bottom, the No.1 smooth plane, 5½" long; the No.3 smooth plane, 8" long; the No. 5 jack plane, 14" long; and the No. 8 jointer, 24" long.*

SCRAPER

Scrapers are used to smooth a board to a tight-textured, glasslike surface, as opposed to the more open-grained surface achieved by sandpaper, which breaks and raises the wood fibers. The Stanley No. 80 is a good example of this type of tool, which was to be found in almost every woodworker's toolbox. Other more sophisticated versions are the Stanley 112 with a vertical handle, and the Stanley 12½ with a horizontal handle (Fig.150). Hand scrapers were made by many manufacturers and some are quite decorative (Fig.151).

Fig.150 *Top left, the Stanley No. 12½ veneer scraper. Top right, the Stanley No. 112 scraper plane. Bottom, the Stanley No. 80 cabinet scraper.*

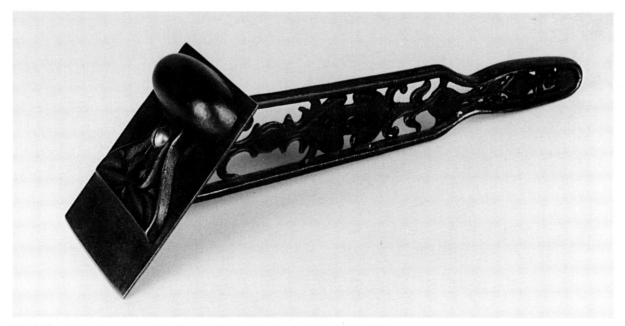

Fig.151 *A hand scraper. The Joseph T. Boufford patent, May 18, 1899.*

CIRCULAR PLANE

Mechanically, these are very intriguing planes. Highly useful, they have flexible adjustable soles, so they can plane a convex or concave surface, varying in arc. Shown in Fig.152 is the Stanley No.113.

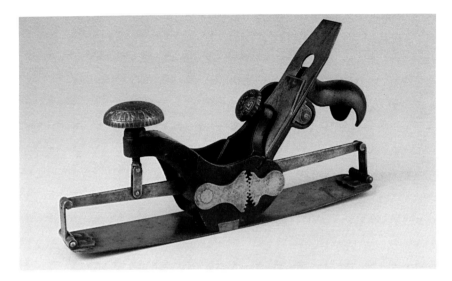

Fig.152   The Stanley No. 113 adjustable circular plane.

BLOCK PLANE

Almost everyone owns a block plane. Even the apartment dweller has one in the kitchen drawer. True, it is usually not sharp enough to do any accurate work, but occasionally a door sticks and has to be planed down. The variety of types, and the numbers of manufacturers making them, provide the collector with a treasure trove of inexpensive collectibles. Blade adjustment is usually the key difference between most types. The angle the blade strikes the work (pitch) is probably the only reason a craftsman would have more than one block plane. The common pitch for block planes (20°) is shown in the Stanley No. 120, while the lower angle pitch (12°), Stanley No. 60½, is used more for cutting against the grain (Fig.153).

Fig. 153   Two Stanley block planes. Above, the No.120; below, the No. 60½.

DADO PLANE

The iron dado plane functions exactly as does the wooden variety. Shown in Fig.154 is the Stanley No. 39 for ½" grooves. There are eight No. 39s, all different widths for different size grooves. The ¹³⁄₁₆" size is generally agreed to have been made from the casting for the ⅞" size, with the 7/8 raised numerals milled off. In this case the box (which is marked ¹³⁄₁₆") is a strong verifier of this exceptionally rare model. Although original boxes improve the value of any production plane, no others can match the value of this box.

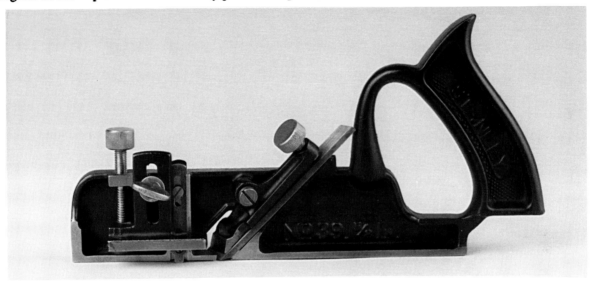

Fig.154 *The Stanley No. 39 dado.*

PLOW and COMBINATION PLANE

These were, and probably always will be, the royalty of the metal plane kingdom, and a woodworker's most prestigious tool will most likely be his plow or combination plane. Those designated as plows merely cut a groove, while the combination planes cut grooves, rabbets, and various molding forms. The most common combination plane (worldwide) is the Stanley No. 45, shown in Fig.155. This is the classic form, originating in 1884 and still used extensively today, although production stopped in 1962. Other companies produced similar planes and some even looked identical, but none received the distribution that the Stanley 45 enjoyed.

Not satisfied with its success with the "45", Stanley offered the ultimate in combination planes, the No. 55 (Fig.156). It had more adjustments, more blades, more fences, more everything. Although many woodworkers give this plane high praise, we have seen too many 55s with almost no usage. There appears to be an inverse relationship between the percentage of "mint" tools to be seen of any particular model and the effectiveness of that model. The 55s were not accepted to anywhere near the degree that the 45s were, probably because of the 55's weight and complexity (6 lbs working weight, with 55 standard cutters and as many optional cutters). But they were the ultimate, and that fact probably was enough to keep them in production.

There is a large price differential between well-used examples with very few cutters left and ones with every last blade, complete with the box, instruction book, and screwdriver. It helps to learn what "complete" means before setting out to buy one of these combination planes.

Although they are not so common, you might run into the Siegley combination plane in almost any tool auction (Fig.157). This plane is a good example of different varieties within a style. It's hard to find two exactly alike.

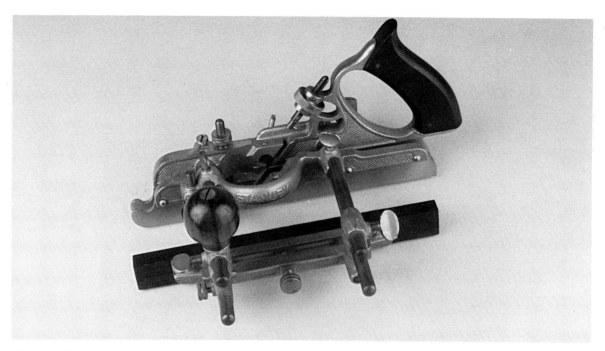

Fig.155   *The Stanley No. 45 combination plane.*

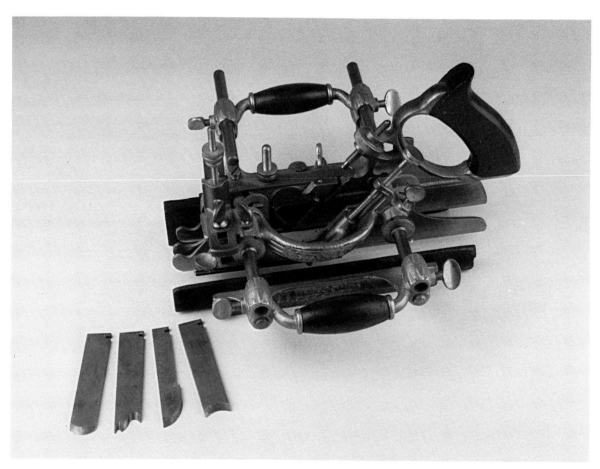

Fig.156   *The Stanley No. 55 Universal combination plane shown with several of the 55 cutters that came with it.*

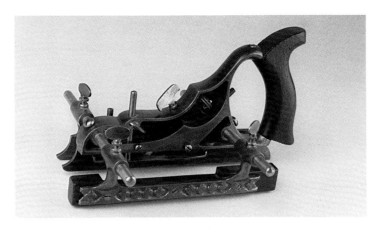

Fig.157   The Siegley combination plane.

This is a good place to bring up an interesting aspect of tool collecting (also found in other collectibles) known as "parts cannibalism," i.e., the removal of parts from an inferior example to complete a similar one that is in better condition. This is common practice and in some instances it was even done by the factory, when left over parts from the previous model were used on the new models just coming off the production line. There are planes today that defy proper dating because of the intermingling of the parts at the factory. And if that isn't confusing enough, many a user has added mismatched parts to keep his tool usable. The final indignity occurred when the collector "restored" the missing parts with other mismatches. It has only been during the past few years that we have begun to understand how mixed up some of these combination planes are. The good news is that this increased knowledge has helped to restore parts to their proper places.

TONGUE AND GROOVE PLANE

The tongue and groove, or swing fence plane, is shown in Fig.158. We can imagine it was used quite a bit since its introduction in 1875, as it was a handy way to cut both the tongue and the groove with one plane. The No.147, which came out later, was not as popular even though it was cheaper at the time (Fig.158).

Many metals tools were japanned (coated with a pigmented varnish, usually black, and then baked). The early models of the No.49 were japanned, but around 1898 the finish was changed to nickel plate. This is an example of how the finish on tools can often be useful in dating the tool. In general, japanned tools are more valuable than their nickel plated younger cousins. Many tools that have lost their japanning are repainted and never really look right. Some are truly re-japanned but are too new looking. There is just no substitute for the real thing.

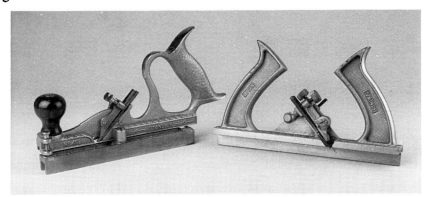

Fig.158   On the left, the Stanley No. 49 tongueing and grooving plane; on the right, the Stanley No. 147 double end match plane.

ROUTER

The wooden routers are highly individualized, most often made by the woodworker for his own use. Among metal planes one design, the Stanley No. 71 (Fig.159) emerged and predominated. It is found everywhere, sometimes with a wood sole added.

Fig.159   *The Stanley No. 71 router plane.*

RABBET PLANE

The rabbet plane evolved in the metal era in two basic styles. The handled Stanley No.78 (Fig160) is still sold today by companies that have duplicated Stanley's design. The single blade can be used in the forward position as a bullnose (cutting close to the edge of a corner), or in the rear position as a rabbet or filletster. There is also a series of handled rabbets that vary in width but have no fences. A typical example is the No.181 (Fig.160).

The design of the unhandled models were patterned after English planes (covered in the English metal plane section). The Stanley No.92 (Fig.160) is an example of this type. As these planes are no longer offered by Stanley, it is important to distinguish between the collectible Stanley models and the contemporary ones. The Stanley name will either be cast into the plane body or on the adjusting knob, or it can be found on a disk in the nose of the plane.

MINIATURE

There are a few frequently found Stanley planes that were made for modelmakers and patternmakers. Some were duplicated by other manufacturers and offered as toys. Although most of these have no markings that would indicate the manufacturer, the Stanley models were good enough to be used by the professionals, while the copies were usually of poor quality. Shown in Fig.161 are examples: the Stanley No.101 block plane, the No.75 bullnose rabbet plane, and the No.100½ block plane, often referred to affectionately as the "squirrel's tail." There were a variety of very tiny planes used by instrument makers that were usually cast in brass.

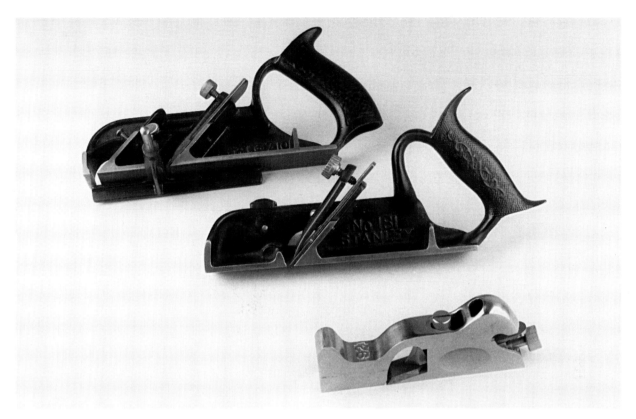

Fig.160 *Top: Stanley No. 78 duplex rabbet plane. Center: Stanley No. 181 rabbet plane. Bottom: Stanley No. 92 cabinet maker's rabbet plane.*

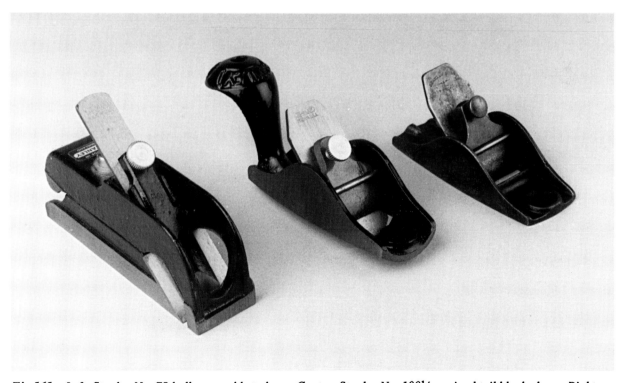

Fig.161 *Left: Stanley No. 75 bull nose rabbet plane. Center: Stanley No. 100½ squirrel tail block plane. Right: Stanley No. 101 block plane, 3½" long.*

SHAVES

Metal spokeshaves have both straight and hollow blades, sometimes both on the same shave. Miniature brass shaves used in instrument making are made, and sold in catalogs, today. It is easy to confuse them with the older, more valuable ones, particularly if the newer brass is deliberately "aged"(Figs.162 and 163).

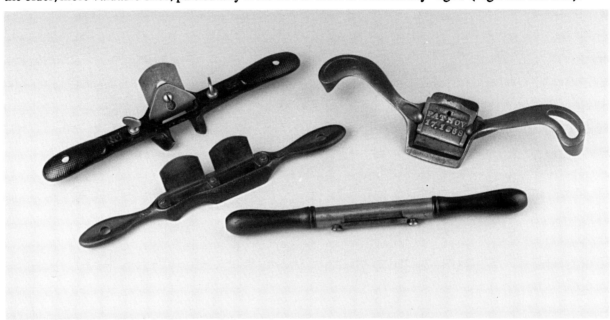

Fig.162 *Various types of shaves. Top left: Stanley No. 65 adjustable chamfer shave; bottom left: Stanley No. 60 double shave; bottom right: Miller's Falls patent Feb.19, 1884.*

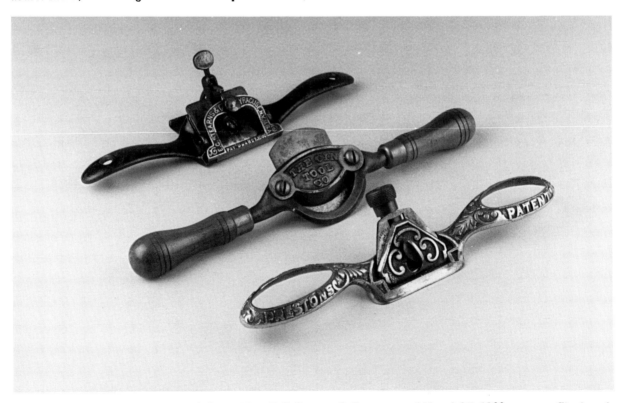

Fig.163 *Some decorative patented shaves. Top: E.C. Stearns & Co., patented March 27, 1900; center: Cincinnati Tool Co.; bottom: Preston's patent.*

METAL BEADERS

Similar to the wooden Windsor beader, the Stanley No.66 beader cuts single or multiple beads of varying sizes (Fig.164).

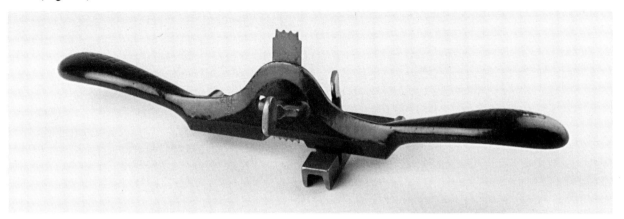

Fig.164   Stanley No. 66 beader.

ENGLISH METAL PLANES

Though the English made and used mass produced metal planes that were much like the American types, they also produced some different varieties that are sought after even today for their high quality, precision workmanship and visual appeal. Two major characteristics make these planes different. First, they have a cast frame made of iron, brass or bronze (or a variation called gunmetal). Second, the frame is "infilled" or "stuffed" with such woods as mahogany, rosewood, or ebony. In the highest quality examples, the iron sole of the plane is dovetailed to the metal body, often so exactly that the dovetails are almost invisible. These planes are generally available in six different styles:

SMOOTHING PLANE

These planes have two basic types of body styles: straight-sided and coffin-shaped; and two types of handles: open and closed, and were also made unhandled (Fig.165).

Fig.165   Two English stuffed smoothing planes, handled and unhandled.

PANEL and JOINTER PLANE

These are somewhat similar to regular jack and jointer planes, ranging in size from 13" to 27". All have closed handles (Fig.166). They are filled in a similar way to the smoothers and many have dovetailed soles. They are still in demand by many woodworkers because of their weight, which tends to hold the plane "to the cut," particularly on cross grain. Norris is the most sought-after manufacturer, especially with those planes that have the patented blade adjustment.

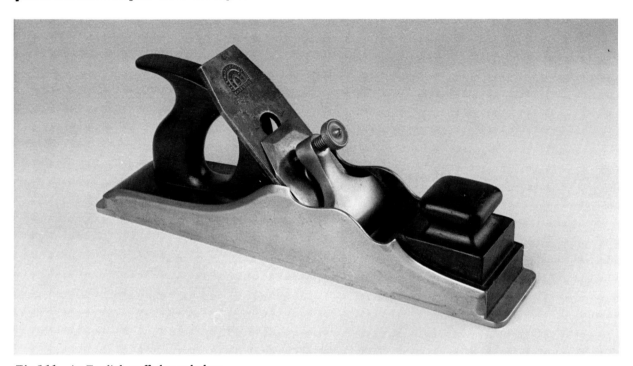

Fig.166   An English stuffed panel plane.

SHOULDER PLANE

These planes have all the characteristics of those mentioned above, except that they have no wooden handles or front knobs and are much narrower. Their wedges, however, are always wood (Fig.167). They are used for rabbeting and cleaning shoulders. The more desirable models were cast in brass or gunmetal.

BULL-NOSE PLANE

Although very much like the shoulder planes, the bull-noses have the added advantage of being able to cut further into a corner because of the forward position of the blade. Bull-nose planes are always shorter than shoulder planes, but, like them, are cast in iron, brass, or gunmetal (Fig.167).

CHARIOT PLANE

The chariot planes were the forerunners of the block planes of today. They show the creativity of the English planemakers, as no two castings are really alike (Fig.167). Their appealing shapes and sizes make them favorites among collectors.

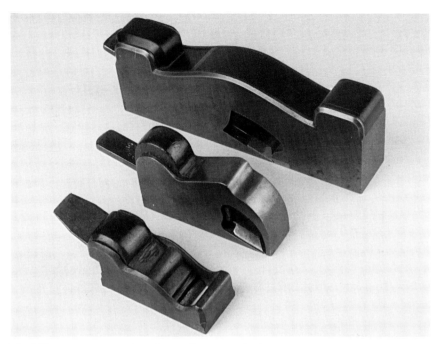

Fig.167 Top: a shoulder plane. Center: a bull nose plane. Bottom: a chariot plane.

MITER PLANE

The English miter planes, because of their extra weight, low angle set of the iron, and very narrow mouth opening (Fig.168), are able to do amazing precision work in cross grain. Most are dovetailed and, like most miter planes, are the only planes in which the iron is set with the cutter bevel up.

Fig.168 English miter planes. The plane at the bottom right clearly shows the dovetailing of the sole to the body.

MEASURING TOOLS

The ability to measure, like the ability to create written records, is fundamental to any organized society. In ancient times one of the most important functions of government was to establish and enforce a uniform system of weights and measures. Without these, the sale and transfer of land, the determination and payment of taxes, the development of trade, and the payment for goods and services could not proceed.

Today we have come to expect uniformity in measurement, together with great accuracy, culminating in the use of laser beams and the atomic clock. It was not always so. The pleasure and intellectual challenge derived from collecting and studying measuring tools comes not only from their aesthetic appeal and mechanical ingenuity, but also because the development of measuring tools so closely mirrors the development of our industrial society.

In the pages that follow, we'll cover the various categories of measuring tools: rules, levels and plumb bobs, squares and bevels, calipers, dividers and compasses, gauges and slitters, and travelers.

RULES

The oldest known rule (in the Cairo Museum) has been traced back to 2600 B.C., though this doesn't necessarily date the inception of measurement.

The Egyptian rules were mostly of wood or stone, and generally one cubit (approximately 1½ feet) in length. The biblical cubit was designated as the distance from the fingertip to the elbow. Continuing the analogy, Egyptian rules were further divided into palms (about 3" long) and each palm into four digits.

The Romans and Greeks had well established measuring units, using a human foot as their basis. Although most of their rules were wood, some were bronze and were even hinged.

With the fall of the Roman empire, uniformity of measure was lost as the succeeding political entities created and attempted to maintain their own particular standards. At the beginning of the 19th century most large cities in Europe had their own standards of measure. Books were published listing all foreign measures to aid travellers and merchants. Another approach to the problem was the development of the comparative rule, which often had four, or sometimes as many as eight, different linear standards on its sides and edges. Each standard was marked for the city or province using it. With the rule, a user could measure and convert directly, rather than go through cumbersome calculations.

Some of the measurements used in 18th century England were:

INCH = 3 barleycorns. The barleycorn has continued to be the basis of shoe measurement, i.e. each shoe size is one barleycorn different from the next.

HAND = 4 inches. The hand is still used today for measuring the height of horses.

SPAN = 9 inches (relating to the span of the hand).

FOOT = 12 inches

CUBIT = 18 inches (fingertip to elbow)

YARD = 36 inches (extended fingertip to nose)

FATHOM = 72 inches (extended fingertip to fingertip)

ELL = generally around 36". Used to measure cloth. There are over 200 recorded different lengths for ells that were used throughout Europe.

Down through the ages, the most common material for rules has been wood, and in the last few hundred years predominantly boxwood. This species has an easy-working, tight grain that resists splitting, is easy to stamp, its light color contrasts well with the black markings, and it has high stability. Steel and brass has been used where durability is paramount (e.g. blacksmithing rules), and ivory in the most expensive rules for its rich decorative effect (though fragile and unable to take hard use). Today, however, with the scarcity of quality boxwood, most rules are being made of "hardwood," steel, or brass.

Rules were generally jointed (hinged) so as to fold up to 6" in length. Therefore, a one foot rule would have two sections or folds (i.e. one hinge) and a two foot rule would have four folds (3 hinges). The joints were almost always brass, with German silver being used on the higher priced models. (German silver, though having the appearance of silver, is really an alloy of copper, nickel and zinc.) The hinges varied in shape from round to square to the more decorative arch. The more expensive rules had their edges trimmed (bound) with brass or German silver, making for a longer lasting and better looking rule. The numbers on early rules were hand struck, but by the early 19th century, machines were developed to alleviate this burdensome task. The earlier rules, because of their individuality and the occasional errors made in consecutive numbering, have great appeal.

Aside from rarity, rules are valued for:

1. Readability — rules naturally tend to show the heaviest wear on the outer side of their folds. On some, particularly the ivory ones, outside markings can be totally illegible. This is a major detraction.

2. Tightness — although the joints must move freely, the folds should stay in place when positioned. Slight snugness is best.

3. Color — yellowing in ivory is a natural sign of age, but if it affects the clarity, it detracts. Stains in boxwood are almost impossible to remove, and detract from value.

4. Straightness — warpage is often found and is obviously undesirable.

5. Original condition — missing parts such as rivets, trim or alignment pins will reduce value, as will cracks. Original finish (e.g. lacquer or varnish) is an asset.

6. Joints - generally, the larger and more ornate the joint, the more valuable the rule.

7. Maker's name — some makers are far more collectible than others.

CARPENTER'S RULE

Most rules used by carpenters were for the day to day task of measuring boards. These rules came in a number of styles, varying basically in length, width, number of folds, trim, type of joint and number of segments to the inch (Fig.169). The six-foot rule was last to be developed. It folds up in two distinct ways: either "zigzag" or "interlock" (Fig.170). The latter style has the added advantage of being able to measure accurately *inside* dimensions as with window and door frames.

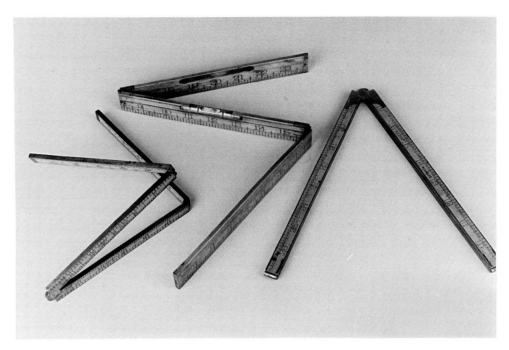

Fig.169   General purpose folding rules. From right to left: two, three, and four fold.

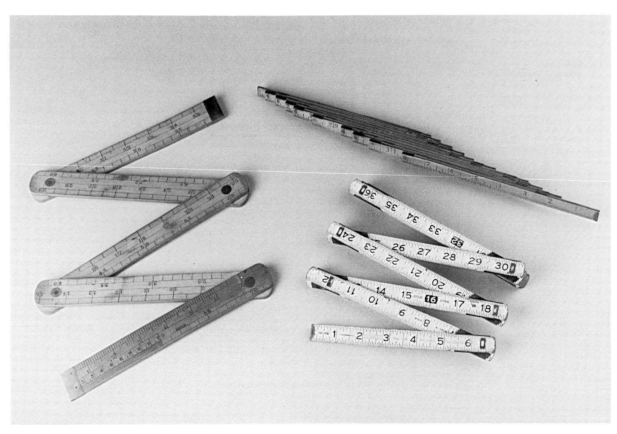

Fig.170   A European zig-zag rule on the left; an American rule on the lower right. Upper right is an interlock rule.

LUMBER RULE

These rules were made specifically for converting the volume of boards, timbers, logs, and even standing trees into a standard measure called a board foot, which is the common measure by which lumber is sold. The classic board foot is a piece 1" thick, 12" wide and 12" long. However any combination of 144 cubic inches is a board foot.

Board rules have a series of scales, each relating to a particular length, e.g. 8', 10' etc., and are used to measure sawn boards. The width of the board is lined up on the scale corresponding to the board length. The board footage for a 1" thick board is read directly from the rule at this position. Some rules are flat and some octagonal. The scales are on all sides and edges.

Log rules, used to measure timber "in the log," are very similar to board rules except the rule takes into consideration the different variables arising when cutting a board from the log, e.g., material lost due to the saw cut and the taper of the log. Some log rules omit the last digit of any marking to save space. The estimator merely adds a zero to each reading when tallying.

Cruising sticks are even more complex. They are used by the forester to determine the volume of standing trees. Basically the user estimates the tree height and the diameter of the tree 4½" above the ground. The stick does the rest.

The biggest improvement for the user came when lumber rules were made flexible with a metal tab extending from one end and a handle on the other. It was now possible to flip the boards around with the rule, rather than having to bend over or to use a handhook. Also the measuring could be done in an upright stance, as the stick flexed almost in a quarter circle. (Figs.171,172,and 173).

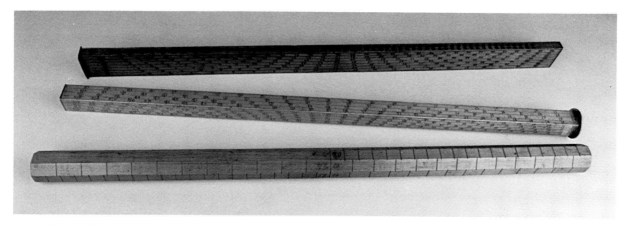

Fig.171   Early lumber rules.

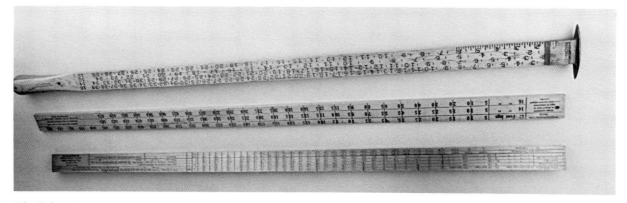

Fig.172   Contemporary lumber rules.

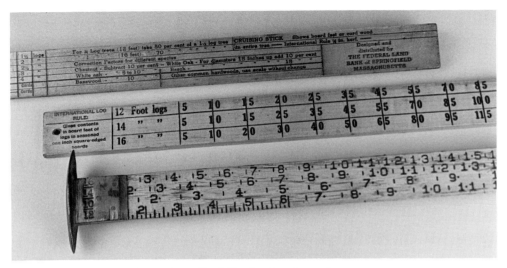

Fig.173   Detail of lumber rules in Fig.172, showing the scales.

PATTERNMAKER'S or SHRINKAGE RULE

One of the characteristics of castings is that the molten metal which is used shrinks when it cools. Therefore the wooden patterns used to form the moldings have to be made slightly larger — based upon the shrinkage rate of the metal being cast. To prevent the patternmaker from having to convert every dimension, the shrinkage rule does it for him by making the rule appropriately oversized. Rules vary in shrinkage rates from ⅟₁₆" per foot to ⅜" per foot and are so identified. They come in at least 10 sizes but complete sets are rare.

ENGINEER'S RULE

These are often very complicated particularly since operating knowledge of many of them has been lost. They have a great variety of scales, slides, and tables, dealing with all manner of materials and industries (Fig.174). The Gunter rule (named after its inventor) is one of these. It plots a logarithmic scale in a straight line and is the forerunner of the modern slide rule (Fig.175).

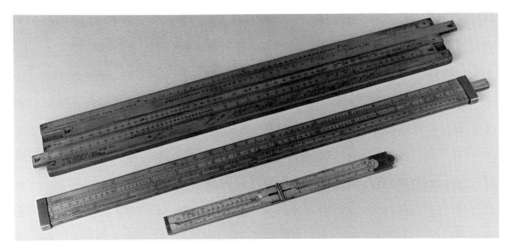

Fig.174   Engineer type rules. Top, Tomlinson's equivalent paper slide scale. Center, a slide rule by Dolland (London) with girt line and inverted line. Bottom, a four fold architect's rule.

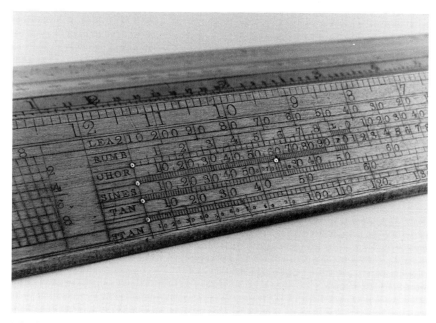

Fig.175   *Detail of a Gunter rule.*

NAVIGATIONAL RULE

There are a great many tools and instruments used in navigation. We will confine ourselves to the simpler "charting" tools, namely the parallel rules, the map rules, and the sector rules.

Although Galileo developed the sector rule (Fig.176) around 1600 as a general purpose calculator (interestingly, it can compute compound interest), it is most often found with navigational equipment. One of its prime uses was to divide any given line into any number of equal parts.

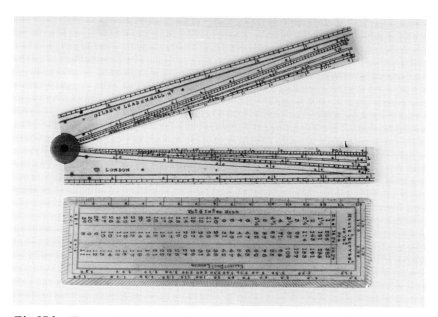

Fig.176   *Top, an ivory sector. Bottom, an ivory map rule. Both are early 19th century English.*

Map rules have scales facilitating map making and map reading (Fig.176). They have a wide range of sizes, but the most common is about 6" long.

Parallel rules, despite their name, are used for plotting parallel lines and not for measuring. Though discussed under navigational rules, they were also used in other occupations such as drafting. The more usual style is hinged as in Fig.177 and usually is made of ebony. The rarer type has rollers that allow the rule to move in a true parallel manner (Fig.178). When ebony became scarce, "ebonized," or blackened, boxwood or maple was used instead. The ebonized wood can usually be detected by lighter colored wear spots, mostly on the edges.

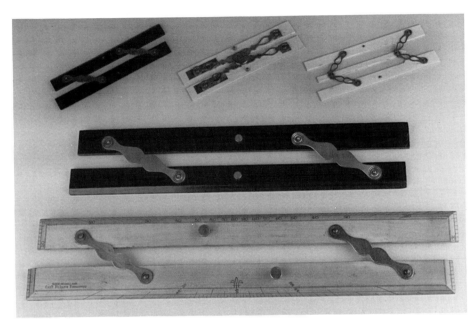

Fig.177   Parallel rules. The bottom rule, imprinted "Capt. Field's Improved," was designed for use in navigation.

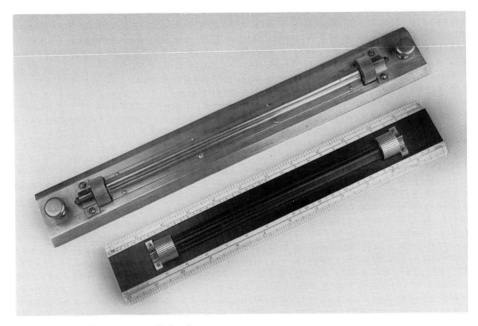

Fig.178   Roller type parallel rules.

CALIPER RULE

These rules have a sliding arm that can accurately measure thickness or diameter. They are useful to carpenters when thickness is critical (Fig.179). They were also used by rope and wire cable makers in determining diameter, and often have an advertising message on them since they were given out by the manufacturer to customers.

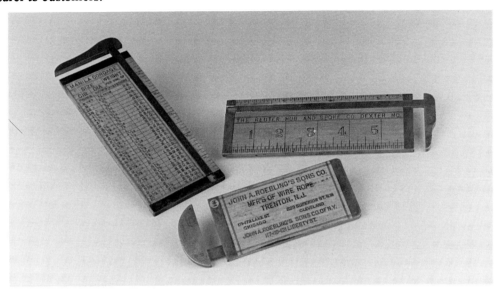

Fig.179 *Caliper rules.*

WANTAGE RULE and GAUGING ROD

An entire industry (alcoholic spirits) at one time depended upon these rules to determine volume and consequently the amount of tax to be paid. Many of these rules still have the government tax branch stamped on the tool or on the case. Some were solid rods, some were hinged, and others were sectional, to be screwed together before use (Figs.180 and 181). Although they functioned like dipsticks (measuring the level of the liquid), it wasn't quite that simple. Barrels came in all sizes (from small firkins to huge hogsheads), but unlike a cylinder, had the added dimension of vertical curvature, which had to be reckoned with. Like the log rules, wantage rules with their tables and scales handled these variables without forcing the measurer to calculate "longhand." Gauging rods only measured depth.

TAILOR'S RULE

Although the right angle shape is very common for tailor's rules, a curved shape is also shown in Fig.182. Sometimes a series of narrow straight rules would represent each suit size. The patented model in Fig.182 had various paper scales clipped to the outer edges, giving the tailor the convenience of one rule. In some of the right angle models, the legs folded together for easier transportability.

ARCHITECT'S RULE

This is an aesthetically pleasing rule that has all the inside folds beveled similar to a school ruler (and for the same purpose, to make it easier to draw a straight line). On these beveled sides are the various scales for architectural drafting.

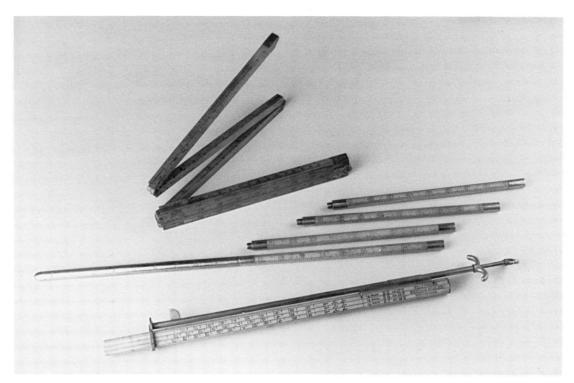

Fig.180 Top, a hinged wantage rule. Center, a screwed-together sectional gauging rod. Bottom, the *Elis Primes 1878 patented wantage scales.*

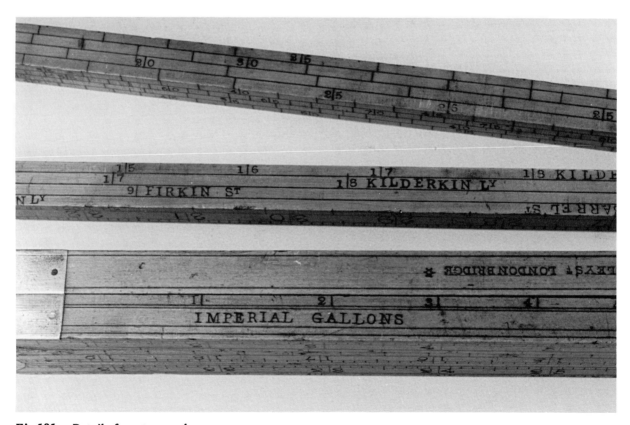

Fig.181 Detail of wantage scales.

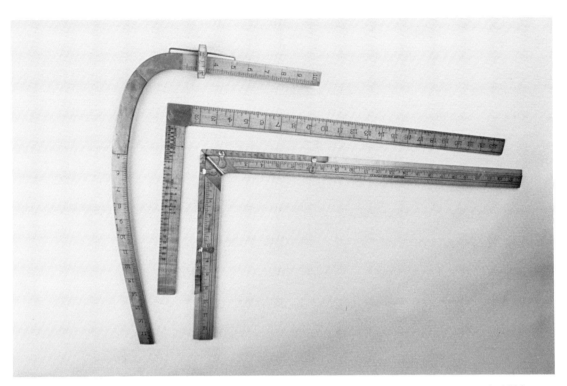

Fig.182   Tailor's rules. Bottom, S.T. Taylor patent. Center, King of Squares, patent Nov. 9, 1880.

COMBINATION RULE

As Will Rogers never met a man he didn't like, we have yet to meet a tool collector who doesn't like the combination rule. The model shown in Fig.183 combines a rule with an inclinometer and a level. Others combine rules, bevels, squares, levels, even a compass (Fig.184).

Fig.183   Combination rule made by the Chapin-Stephens Co.

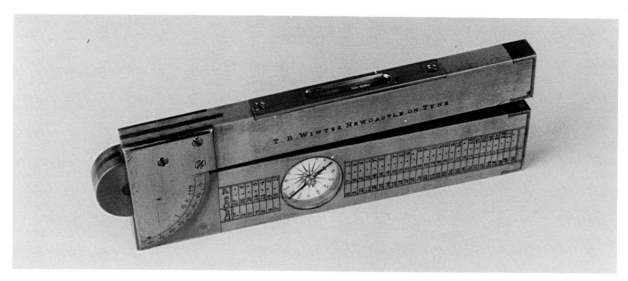

Fig.184   An English combination rule that even includes a compass.

OTHER RULES

There is a rule for almost every measuring purpose. A few of these are shown in Figs.185 through 188.

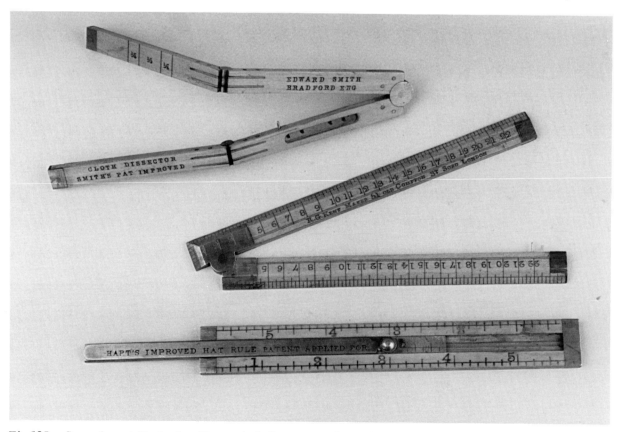

Fig.185   Several specialized rules. Top, a cloth dissector used to make a thread count in fabrics. Center, a pocket square. Bottom, a hat measure.

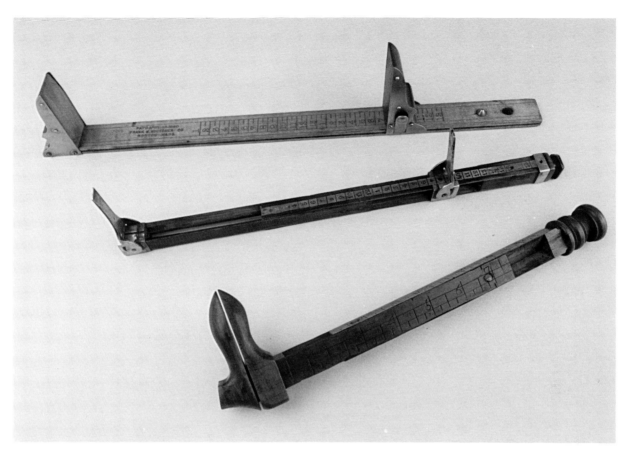

Fig.186   Various foot measures.

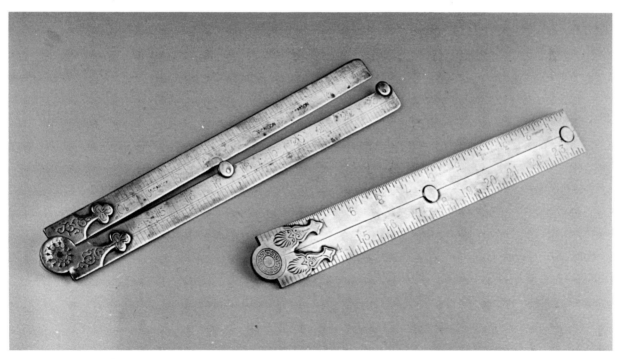

Fig.187   Brass rules by the English maker, Rabone.

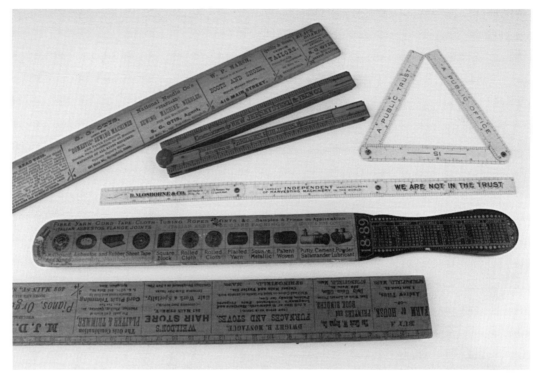

FIg.188   *Advertising rules.*

LEVELS AND PLUMB BOBS

A level is used to determine whether an object is either parallel (level) to the earth's surface, or perpendicular (plumb) to it.

Leveling with a plumb bob dates back to the Egyptians. It consists of hanging a weight on a string to yield a plumb line. The level surface is then at right angles to the plumb line.

PLUMB BOBS

Plumb bobs are made of a variety of materials: brass, bronze, iron, steel, lead, and sometimes wood. The wooden ones are rare and are often confused with plumbers' flaring tools, sailors' fids, or even children's spinning tops. Bobs are found in all kinds of shapes and weights (Fig.189). An unusual way of attaching the string is shown in Fig.190, where the string is held in a reel, and can be adjusted to any given length.

Most brass bobs have steel tips which help prevent denting of the softer material. Some are hollowed and filled with mercury to provide a low center of gravity to steady the bob into a final rest position.

The biggest variation is in weight, ranging from 1½ ounces to 5 pounds. This difference is required to satisfy the various "drop" distances. A small 3-ounce bob would swing like a pendulum if used on a 50-foot drop off a bridge. And no carpenter hanging a door would want to carry around a 4- pound bob.

Collectors are mostly concerned with shape; most consider the turned examples more valuable than similar cast ones. The hexagonal, cylindrical or cone shapes of modern surveyor bobs (e.g., by Dietzgen or Starrett) don't seem to excite the interest that English and European finial-top shapes do.

Most desirable are the 18th century bobs that take a trained eye to recognize. Plumb bobs are yet another example of tools collected primarily for their aesthetics.

Fig.189   *Some examples of plumb bobs.*

Fig.190   *A reel type plumb bob.*

LEVELS

Leveling can also be done with a bubble of air trapped in a vial of alcohol or other spirits (hence the name spirit level). The vial has a slight curvature so that the bubble will rise to its center when level. The less the curvature the more sensitive the level. The vial is generally shielded in a brass tube, open on one side. The vial and the tube are bonded together with plaster of paris. In many levels, the tube is adjustable with screws so that it can be reset if dropped or when replacing a vial. Although the glass vials are not as fragile as they might seem, they are still the major cause of trouble on antique levels. If they are not completely broken or missing, the fluid has sometimes evaporated out. They are not difficult to replace if you can find the right size vial. If not, the level will be greatly reduced in value, even as a collectible.

CARPENTER'S WOODEN SPIRIT LEVEL

These vary in size from 6" to 30" and are basically as shown in Fig.191. The larger levels are predominantly cherry, mahogany or rosewood, with the smaller ones using the above woods plus boxwood and ebony. These smaller ones are quite showy at times, particularly the English and Scottish ones made from ebony with inlaid brass (Fig.192).

The stocks were picked for straight grain and stability and sometimes laminated to prevent warpage. The ends of the better levels have brass plates for protection, and on the premier models all four edges are "bound" with brass strips. There is a top brass plate protecting the vial and, many times, brass side view plates on either side of the vial. Most levels also have plumb vials, i.e., the bubble is at right angles to the central bubble. With this feature, the user could plumb a wall, pillar or post for true verticalness.

There are a series of brass edge-bound levels made by Stratton Bros. and the Stanley Co. in various sizes, using mostly rosewood or mahogany. Because the smaller levels had a more limited use than the larger ones, they are rarer. The Stratton 6½" and the Stanley 6" are the rarest of the series.

Fig.191   Carpenter's wooden spirit levels.

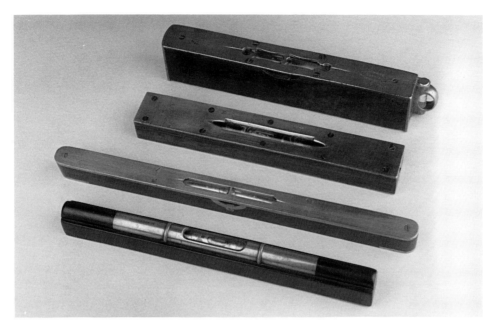

Fig.192 *Fancy English levels.*

CARPENTER'S CAST IRON SPIRIT LEVEL

As the name implies, these levels have their bodies cast in iron, with vials and tubes screwed to the bodies. Many of these have very ornate designs, typical of the Victorian era (Fig.193). The Davis Level and Tool Co. inserted inclinometers into machined openings in the body.

Fig.193 *The top two levels are 18" long and made by the Davis Level & Tool Co. The one on the bottom is the Nicholson 1860 patent, but made by the Stanley Rule & Level Co., which had acquired the company.*

The inclinometer utilizes a vial mounted in a circular protractor. When the level is set on an inclined surface, the protractor is turned until the bubble is centered. The degree of inclination is read directly from the protractor. These Davis inclinometer-levels came in a series of sizes, the smallest being the "mantel-clock" model, only 6" overall (Fig.194).

The disadvantage of the cast iron level was its brittleness. If the level was dropped or hit on a corner, a piece would usually break out. A "clean" cast iron level, with no chips, is getting to be the exception rather than the rule.

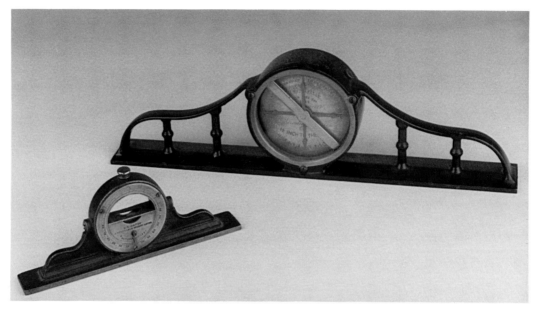

Fig.194   Two interesting leveling devices. Lower left, a Davis Level & Tool Co. 6" level. Right, a W.B. Mellick 1889 patent inclinometer grading scale.

POCKET LEVEL

Stanley, Davis and others made many styles of small pocket sized levels. Some were used directly on the workpiece, while others were attached to a straight edge, square, or line cord (Fig.195).

Fig.195   Some pocket levels ranging between 2" and 4½" long.

MACHINIST'S LEVEL

Although many pocket levels were used by machinists, the more precise machinist level was the mounted style shown in Fig.196. This type carried a very sensitive bubble and had its bottom milled so as to provide the accuracy and close tolerances required. Often, rotating covers protected the glass vials.

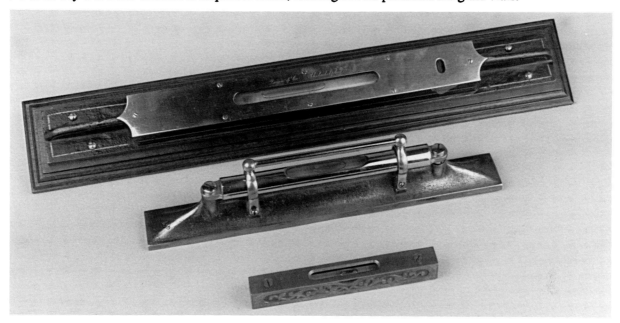

Fig.196 *Machinist's levels.*

RAILROAD LEVEL

A highly specialized form of level was used for railroad grade work. It had sighting devices built into the body so the user could "shoot a grade." It was truly an inclinometer, as it measured the track incline by a gravity dial (Fig.197).

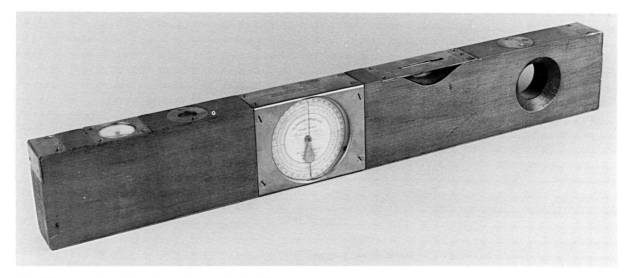

Fig.197 *A railroad level, the Edward Helb 1904 patent.*

MASON'S LEVEL

Most mason's levels are not normally considered collectible, because of their modern look, e.g., aluminum, philippine mahogany, bright paint, etc. There are many of these contemporary models available at flea markets and auctions. They are 36" to 48" long, with at least three bubbles.

The collector will find levels fascinating to collect and restore, as they can be brought back to life with dramatic results. The contrast between the darker woods and the brass is very pleasing, particularly where intricate patterns are involved. There are few tools that display wood grain as well as levels. In many cases the maker deliberately included the lighter sapwood on a corner of the level for contrast. Old levels are sought after by decorators, homeowners, and others who enjoy their aesthetic appeal. Needless to say, they are also one of the favorites of tool collectors.

SQUARES AND BEVELS

Squares and bevels date back at least to the time of the Pharoahs, which is not surprising since the square is an indispensable tool in all types of construction from furniture to buildings and boats.

The try square is used for scribing a line at right angles to the edge of a board, while a miter square functions at 45°. The handle of the square acts as the fence, and the blade becomes the scribing edge. The bevel has the same purpose, except that it is used to scribe a line at *any* angle. Almost all squares are permanently fixed in position; almost all bevels are adjustable.

FRAMING or ROOFING SQUARE

These squares are made of iron or steel. The handforged 18th century ones have handstruck numbers. One leg is longer than the other, with the longer side generally measuring 24" (Fig.198). The later roofing squares have scales that figure the rafter size for various pitches (angle of slant) of the roof.

An interesting version of these squares is called the "take-down" square. It has all the features previously described and, in addition, can be taken down, or separated, at the corner joint, so as to fit more conveniently in the tool box.

Fig.198   On the left and bottom, the two parts of a "take-down" square. On the right, a handstruck square.

TRY SQUARE

This is one of the most common tools found today, as every woodworker needed one. They come in many sizes, ranging from 3" to 18" blades. The inner side of the handle is usually faced with brass and the plates holding the rivets are also brass, sometimes formed into unusual decorative patterns. Rosewood was generally used for the handles, with ebony used for the more expensive models (Fig.199).

In the larger squares, a tab was sometimes set into the lower part of the handle to steady it against the board. Some even have levels in the handle to allow a true vertical plumb line to be scribed.

Fig. 199   Try squares.

MITER SQUARE

There are two types of miter squares, one scribing only at a 45° angle and the other being able to scribe at either 45° or 90° (Fig.200).

Fig.200   45° miter squares.

T-SQUARE

Although the all-wood T-square is used predominantly for drafting, versions of it have found their way into other fields such as glazier work.

BEVEL

A bevel is really a "square" with a moveable blade, allowing it to assume any angle. The T-bevel pivots in the center while the more common sliding bevel has a slot that allows the length of the blade to be adjusted. A variety of clamping features were used on bevels such as a knurled nut, screw, wingnut, or lever. Many of these were patented (Fig.201).

Fig.201   Bevels

SHIPBUILDER'S BEVEL

This bevel was used to scribe compound angles on ship's planks and frame. It consisted of a hardwood stock generally 12" long, graduated in inches, slotted at either end to contain two metal tongues, usually brass, one short and one long (Fig.202). There were also similar bevels with only one tongue.

COMBINATION SQUARE AND BEVEL

These are the premier models of this category, most of them patented. The Richie patent, shown in Fig.203, has a square, a bevel, and two levels. It was produced mostly in mahogany. Fig.204 shows some other combination squares and bevels, proving that even a simple tool can be an exciting collectible.

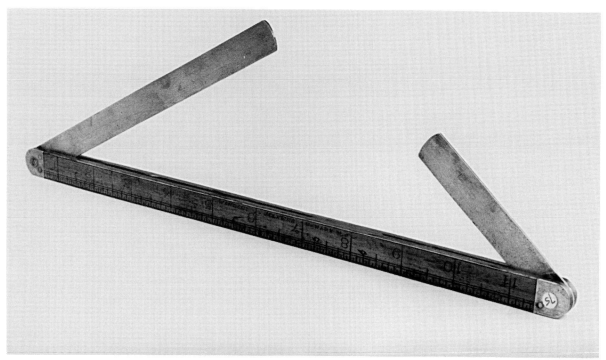

Fig.202 *Shipbuilder's bevel.*

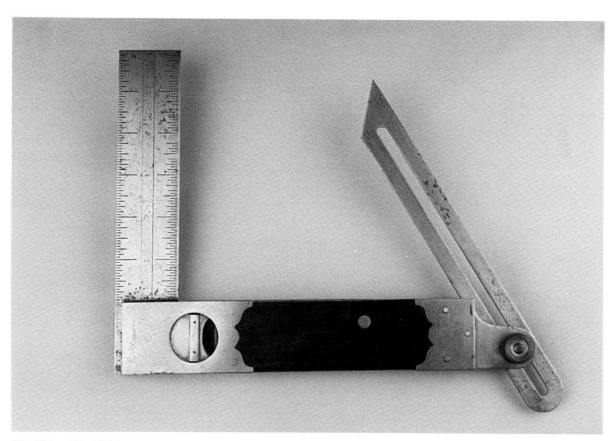

Fig.203 *The Richie patent.*

Fig.204 Some other interesting combination squares and bevel. Top, unmarked. Bottom left, the W.F. Fisher 1868 patent. Bottom right, stamped "Frank H. Coe/Sole Manfgr/Boonton N.J."

CALIPERS, DIVIDERS AND COMPASSES

Though simple appearing, these tools are almost indispensable. They have been with us since Roman times, performing three basic functions:

Calipers...for measuring thickness or diameter.

Dividers...for providing equally spaced points.

Compasses..for scribing circles or arcs.

All three instruments function in somewhat the same manner: either their legs are set apart a predetermined distance and this dimension is transferred to the workpiece, or they are set to an unknown dimension on the workpiece and then measured to determine that dimension.

The legs are kept apart by three techniques: friction, wingnut, or spring. The friction style depends on a tightly fitting hinge to prevent the legs from changing position. The wing style has a nut which clamps on an arm (or wing) and locks the legs in position. The spring style is used for smaller instruments and depends upon the spring action in the metal hinge in conjunction with the wingnut on the screw arm, (Fig.205).

NOTE: One form of the caliper, the caliper rule, which reads the thickness directly on a rule, was included in the section on Rules and will not be repeated here.

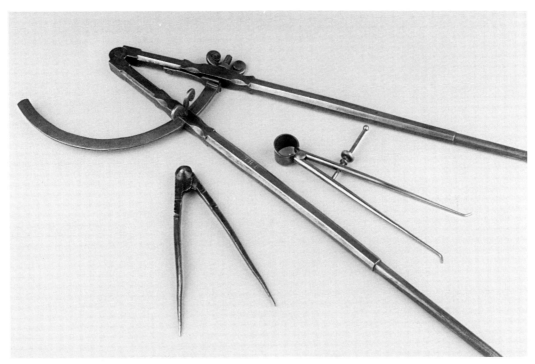

Fig.205 *The three methods of adjusting the legs: from the top, wingnut, spring, and friction.*

OUTSIDE CALIPER

These are the most common type of calipers, and are used to measure a solid or "outside" diameter. In lathe turning, for instance, a caliper would be used to check the dimension of the workpiece against the design or blueprint. Such calipers range from the small machinist models with 4" legs to the wheelwright's and patternmaker's calipers with legs up to 30" in length (Fig.206).

Fig.206 *Outside calipers.*

INSIDE CALIPER

As the name suggests, these are used to measure the inside diameter of holes (Fig.207). They generally range from 4" to 8" in leg length.

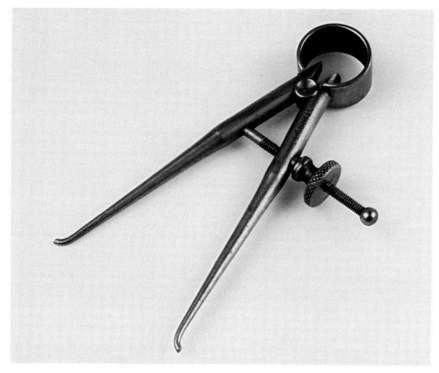

Fig.207   *Inside caliper.*

DOUBLE CALIPER

These can be used to set dimensions for two separate diameters. They also could be used as "go, no-go" gauges for more precise work. By setting one side a hair over the diameter and the other side a hair under, the calipers could assure the finished pieces were within allowable tolerances. Double calipers were almost all hand-forged by blacksmiths. Some of the better-made examples are almost sculptural in appearance and are sometimes used as decorative wall hangings (Fig.208).

DANCING MASTER CALIPER

These calipers are whimsical artforms that were often homemade and reflect the creativity of their makers. Some were shaped in the form of the "dancing legs", while others showed the entire body silhouette (Fig.209).

LOG CALIPER

The lumber industry has given us many dramatic and impressive tools, e.g., pit saws, goosewing axes, log turning pikes and log calipers. These calipers measure the diameter of the log and convert it directly into board feet of lumber based on the length of the log (Fig.210). They work very much like the log rules described previously. However they have one unique feature included only on the premier models: a rotating wheel with 10 protruding pointed spokes at the very end of the beam. The tips of these spokes are 6" apart and are used to measure the log length as the wheel was "walked" along the log. One full rotation of the wheel constitutes 5 feet in log length. The first or "zero" spoke is usually weighted, so it hangs in the proper position to start.

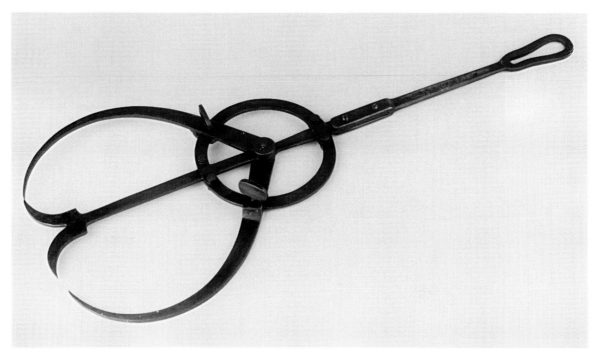

Fig.208   *Double caliper.*

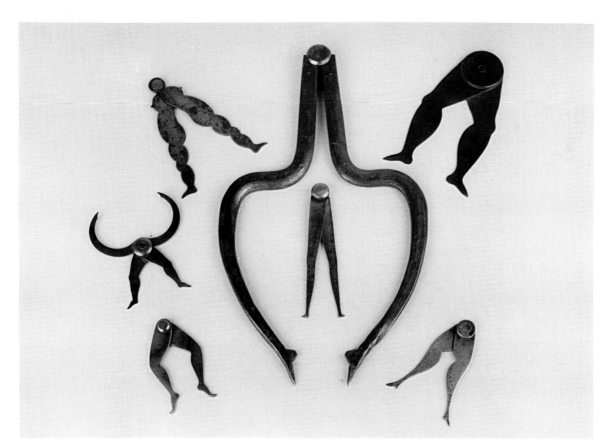

Fig.209   *Dancing master calipers.*

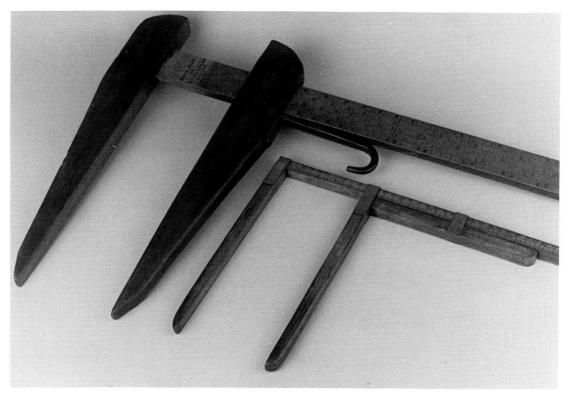

Fig.210   Log calipers.

Most log calipers never had wheels, and many that originally had them now have them missing. And little wonder! If you consider the weight and inconvenience of lugging around this awkward spiked caliper, you will probably agree that we are lucky that *any* wheels remain today. These, like many other ineffective tools, are rare. Log calipers with their original wheels are worth two to three times the value of those without wheels. Because of the dramatic look of the complete "pinwheel" calipers, even another manufacturer's wheel significantly improves the caliper's value, (Fig.211).

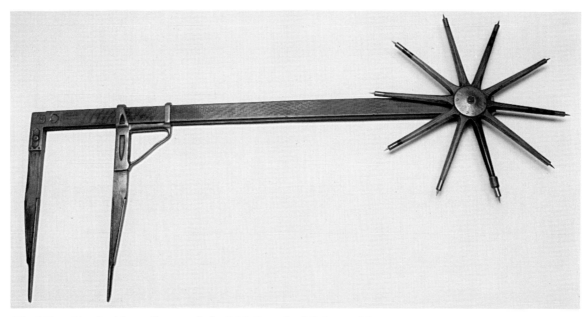

Fig.211   Pinwheel log caliper made by F.M. Greenleaf, Belmont, Mass.

WOODEN DIVIDER

All dividers have straight legs, as their only functions are to divide a dimension into equal parts, or to set up equal spacing between objects (Fig.212). The larger ones (over 2 feet) have great decorative value, aside from being highly collectible. Do not confuse factory-made school chalk compasses with wooden dividers. The latter have steel points on both legs.

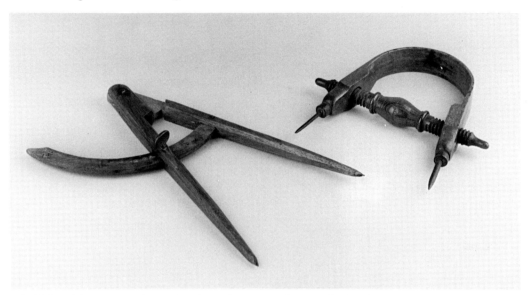

Fig.212   Wooden dividers. On the right, a French cooper's divider.

METAL DIVIDER

These range from the tiny 3½" spring dividers used by draftsmen to the 30" wing dividers used by wheelwrights. One of the types used by coopers is distinguished by its handforged decorative serrations and chamfers. Dividers are often referred to as compasses, and the cooper's divider is just such a case. After using it to divide the circumference of the barrel into six parts, the cooper then used it to scribe the circular lid, using the found dimension as the radius (Figs.213, 214, and 215).

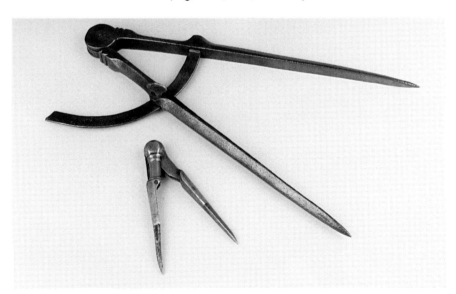

Fig.213   Top, a cooper's divider. Bottom, 18th century European.

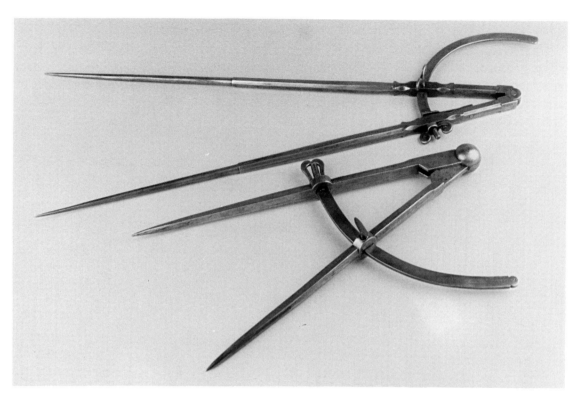

Fig.214 *Two finely made dividers. The one on the top has 22" long legs.*

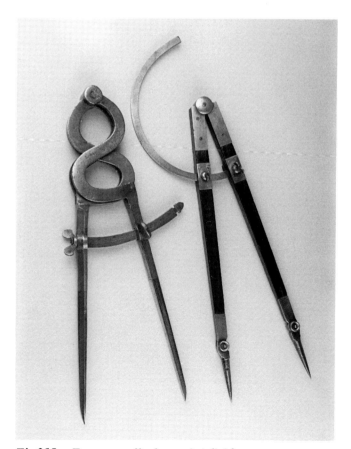

Fig.215 *Two unusually decorative dividers.*

PROPORTIONAL DIVIDER

Fig.216 shows a divider that could scale-down or scale-up any drawing or object merely by varying the pivot point of the "scissors." They are predominantly brass and English-made. Many are found in their original cases.

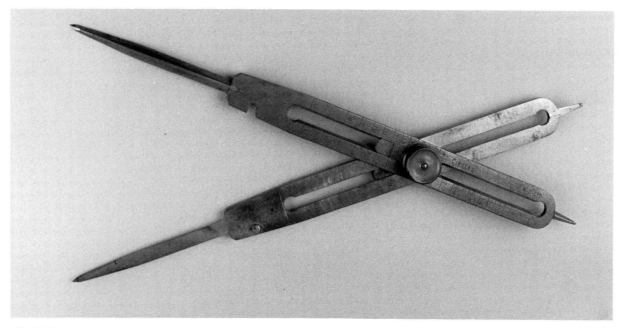

Fig.216 *Proportional divider.*

BEAM COMPASS or TRAMMELS

This compass was used by carpenters, wheelwrights, shipwrights and patternmakers to scribe large circles or arcs. Two scribe points (trammel points), mounted in wooden or metal heads, slide along a wooden beam 2' to 4' long. With one point stationary, the other does the circling. They can also be used as dividers for spacing. The wooden heads are either wedge or thumbscrew locked, while the metal ones were generally ornate brass and locked by thumbscrew only (Fig.217). The craftsman would carry the "points" (heads) with him, but not necessarily the beam. It could be left on the job, and if lost, a new one could easily be made. Most trammel points are found today without the beam.

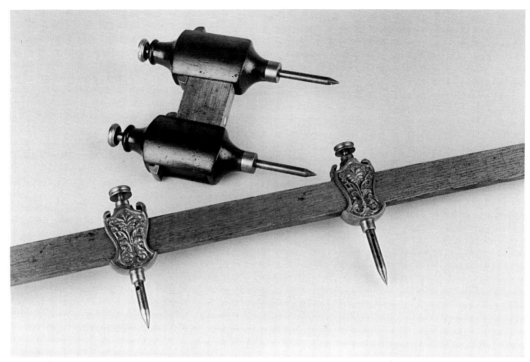

Fig.217   *Beam compass (trammel points). The trammel points on the top are on a "keeper" beam, which is used to hold them while in the tool box.*

GAUGES AND SLITTERS

Although a gauge is technically an instrument for measuring, some liberties were taken when the tools used for marking and slitting were called gauges. Marking gauges and panel gauges scribe a premeasured line parallel to the edge of the board. Mortise gauges scribe two such lines (defining each side of the mortise). Slitters, sometimes called "cutting gauges," cut veneer, thin boards, and leather, usually parallel to the edge. It could be argued that because slitters actually change the form of the product, they should not be included under Measuring Tools. However, this book will group slitters along with gauges because their looks and manner of use are close enough to be considered "family."

Early marking gauges (pre-18th century) did not have a scriber or "spur" integral to the tool. The user held a marker at the end of the stem and had it follow the gauge. Many woodworkers today use an even simpler method of scribing, i.e., they use their last three fingers as the fence, and hold the pencil or scriber at the proper distance from the edge with their thumb and forefinger. Maybe that's how the Egyptians and Romans did it, as there is no record of this kind of tool being used in those eras.

MARKING GAUGE

Many collectors purchase a marking gauge as their first antique tool. They are plentiful, relatively inexpensive, simple in function, and usually attractive. Most of the factory-made ones are trimmed in brass and make a striking contrast with the darker woods that were used: mahogany, rosewood, lignum and ebony, and even with the lighter boxwood. If the gauge was owner- made, it might be from almost any wood. The woods used for this tool were so diverse that some collectors use their marking gauges to illustrate the different species (Fig.218).

Fig.218   Marking gauges.

Most of the factory-made varieties have a screw-locked fence; either a thumb screw or a machine screw. The owner-made ones are almost always wedge-locked. The better gauges have wear strips in the fence and some even have a full brass plate attached to the fence. Stanley and a few other American companies made all-metal gauges but most woodworkers still prefer wooden ones. Although some of the factory-made gauges have fractional inch marks on the stem, most of the homemade ones do not.

There are a few patented models that are relatively valuable. Fig.219 shows the Blaisdell patent for convex and concave work, the Williams patent with four spurs at the end of the stem, and the Scholl patent with three or four independent stems.

MORTISE GAUGE

Very much like the marking gauge, the mortise gauge differs in that it has *two* spurs and can scribe both sides of the mortise length simultaneously. One spur is fixed at the end of the stem (as in the marking gauge) and the other is adjustable by a long screw, or slide, through the stem (Fig.220).

Mortise gauges are mostly made of rosewood, ebony, or boxwood. The English manufactured a classic gauge with a round brass stem and an ebony and brass fence, and a much rarer one with a solid brass fence. Some mortise gauges had *two* fixed spurs on opposite sides of the stem in addition to the adjustable spur. This allowed the gauge to be used for either marking or mortising. Another combination type gauge was the Stanley No. 92 (Fig.221), which was used for scribing the locations of hinges and plates for doors.

There are also some unique types made by wheelwrights and coachmakers called "grasshopper" gauges that utilize the stem as the fence (Fig.222). Mortise gauges come in a great number of configurations. Just when you think you have seen them all, a new style comes along to surprise you.

PANEL GAUGE

These are not much more than longer marking gauges (18"-30") with a step in the fence to provide a better guide against the wide board or panel being marked. Most were homemade, with a wedge- locked fence. Some of them showed a "free-form" type of fence that fit the hand better. There are some manufactured pieces (mostly rosewood) that have brass wear plates and thumbscrew locks (Fig.223).

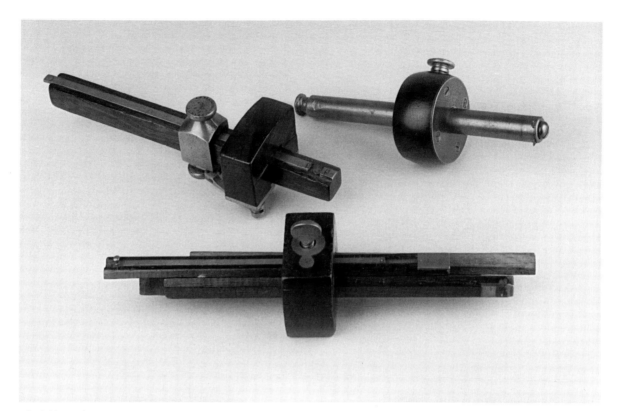

Fig.219 *Three patented marking gauges. Upper left, Blaisdell 1868 patent. Upper right, the Williams patent.*
Bottom, the Scholl 1864 patent.

Fig.220 *Mortise gauges.*

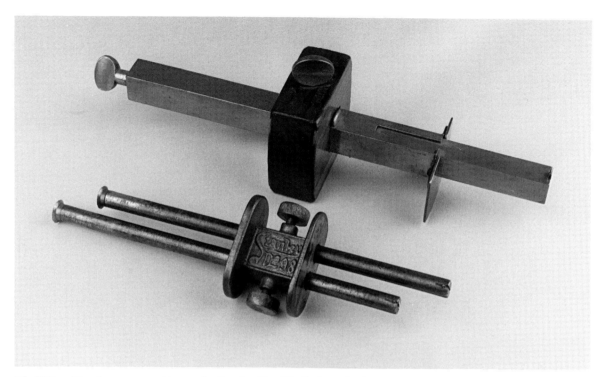

Fig.221 *Mortise gauges. Above, the Stanley No. 92. Below, the Stanley No. 98.*

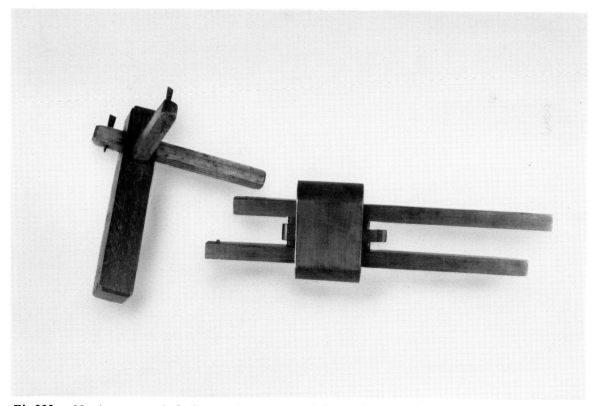

Fig.222 *Mortise gauges. Left, the grasshopper type; right, Continental style..*

Fig.223   *Two panel gauges. Left, tiger maple, owner-made. Right, rosewood factory-made.*

SLITTER

Slitters, as their name implies, slit the work instead of merely scribing it. Instead of a spur, they carry a knife-like blade. Although used mostly for veneer (Fig.224), some of the sturdier models with handles could be used for thin boards such as drawer bottoms (Fig.225). Another variety, a pleasingly shaped leather slitter, used by shoemakers and other leather workers, has rosewood or mahogany inlaid into the brass frame (Fig.226).

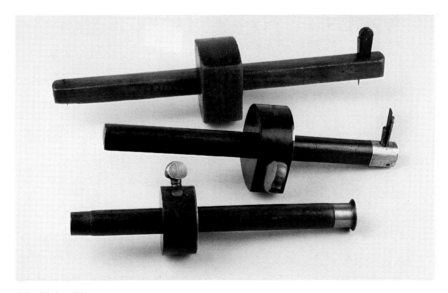

Fig.224   *Slitters*

Fig.225 *A handled slitter.*

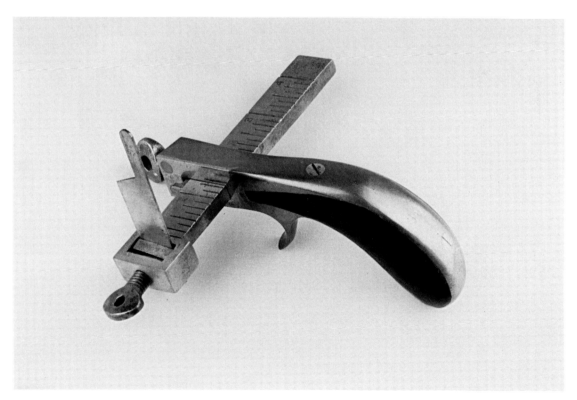

Fig.226 *Leatherworker's slitter.*

TRAVELERS

Travelers were used predominantly in the wheelwright trade to "travel" or roll around the circumference of the rim of a wagon wheel, so as to size the iron "tire" before it was fitted and shrunk on the wheel. The traveler wheel spins on a handle and has the start designated with a mark or hole. Some traveler wheels are marked in inches to make it easier to transfer the exact size from rim to tire. Travelers were made in wood, brass or iron. The wooden types were almost entirely owner-made; the iron ones were forged by blacksmiths, cast by factories, or cut out of sheet metal. They had iron or wooden handles, some with brass ferrules. Most of the factory-made models had a pointer to assist in keeping track of the revolutions (Fig.227).

Decorative handforged travelers command higher prices than iron factory-made ones, but the rarer brass or bronze examples are premier no matter how made. Besides representing an interesting part of our past, they also display beautifully on the wall.

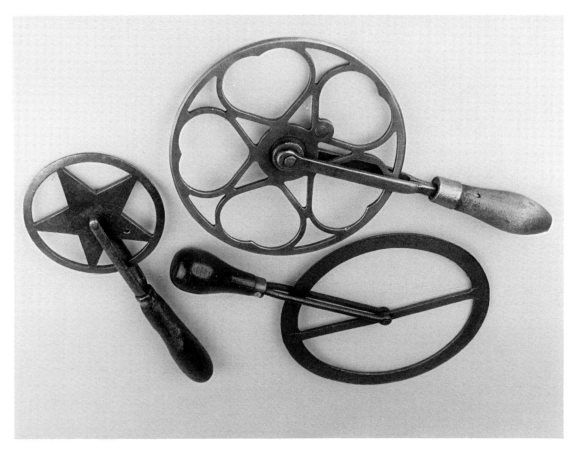

Fig.227   Travelers.

SAWS

Early bronze-bladed saws had to be held in frames to keep the blades from buckling. Iron was not used for saw blades until the Roman era. It was around this Roman period that "set" to the teeth was introduced. Set is the swaging, or bending outward, of the teeth, each tooth being bent in an opposite direction to the one next to it. This provides a wider cutting path (kerf) to enable the blade to clear the sides of the cut without binding (Fig.228).

Most saws are used to cut across the grain. There are still a few notable exceptions: the carpenter's rip saw (see Hand Saw) and the motor-powered circular rip saws used in sawmills and woodshops. The sizes and angles of the teeth are the predominant factors in the various usages of saws. A general rule is that rip saws have the cutting edges of their teeth square to the blade, and cross-cut saws have their teeth angled to the blade (Fig.228). If we think of each tooth as a tiny plane blade, we can readily understand the angular difference. A smooth plane, cutting with the grain, has a blade square to the body; a miter plane, cutting across the grain, has a skewed blade and sometimes knife-like nickers. The smoothness of the sawcut is controlled by the number of teeth per inch: the more teeth, the smoother the cut.

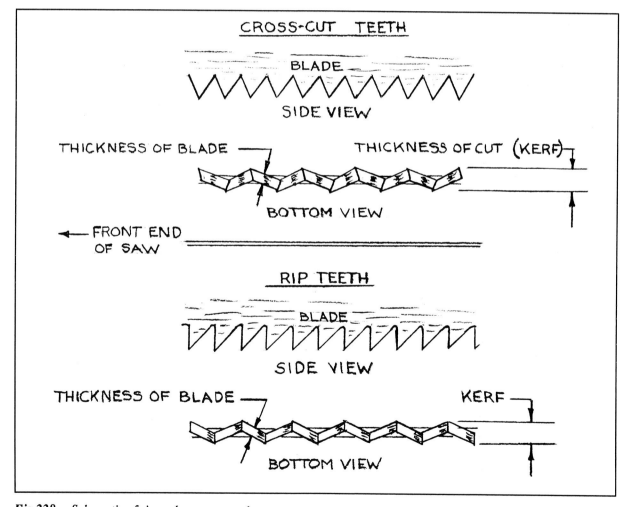

Fig.228   Schematic of rip and crosscut teeth.

TWO-MAN SAWS

CROSS-CUT TIMBER SAW

These large saws (Fig.229) were a boon to early lumbermen, as they allowed the log to be cut to length without the time-consuming and wasteful axework. Saws around 3 feet in length could be used by one man, but the larger ones, approximately 6 feet, required two men. It is interesting to watch lumberman contests in cross-cut sawing. Timing is the key to success, not necessarily strength. With expert timing and feel, one man can actually use a 6 foot saw alone!

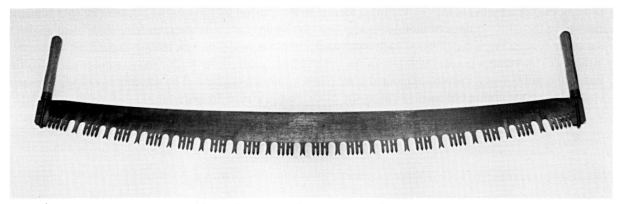

Fig.229   Crosscut timber saw used by lumbermen, timber framers, and farmers.

PIT SAW and PLANK SAW

Where water power, and later steam and gasoline power, was not available, logs were manually cut into boards by sawing down their length with a pit saw. One man stood on top of the log with the "tiller" end of the saw, and the other man (the less fortunate one) was under the log in a pit, pulling downward each time the tillerman brought the blade back up. Much of our early lumber was made in this fashion.

In some areas, the log was dragged up onto a structure; this allowed the pitman to work on level ground. Early pitsaws were contained in a frame. Some were used to cut planks out of already squared up timbers (Fig.230). Later ones were wider and "open" with removable handles (Fig.231). They were approximately seven feet long.

Fig.230   Framed plank saw used by coachmakers, shipwrights, and housewrights.

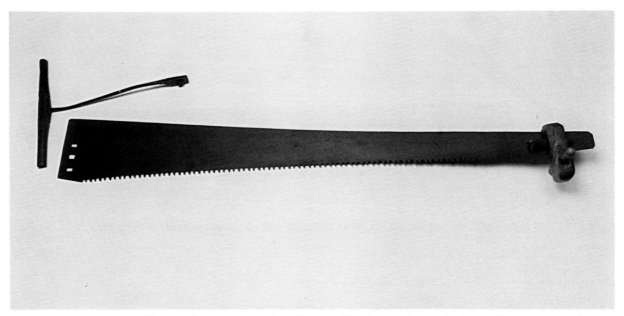

Fig.231 *Open pit saw. The handle on the top left, called the tiller handle, is attached to, and extends out almost parallel to, the blade. The wood handle on the right end of the saw, which is the lower end, is held to the blade with a wooden wedge and is removeable.*

VENEER SAW

Looking in general much like the framed pit saw, the veneer saw had a shorter, thinner and narrower blade, with many more teeth per inch. It was used to cut thin sections of veneer, before rotary-cut machine veneering was developed. Veneer saws had parallel width blades (most all pit saw blades tapered from top to bottom).

ONE-MAN TWO-HANDED SAWS

ICE SAW

Some of us remember the iceman and his quaint horse and wagon, but few are aware of an entire industry that preceded the refrigerator. Ice was cut from ponds and lakes just before the early spring thaw. The blocks were dragged to an ice house, a structure generally cut into the bank where the ground provided the best insulation. The ice was layered with straw and kept its form well into the early fall.

Ice saws are often mistaken for lumber saws. Besides having a shorter blade than the pit saw, the teeth are larger, about 1½" apart, compared with the ½" - 1" spacing of the pit saw. And of course there never is a handle on the end used under the ice (Fig.232).

BUCK SAW

Used for "bucking," or cutting logs and branches to length for pulpwood or firewood, these saws are still a common tool around the farm. As they are used in a horizontal position by one man, they usually have just one handle and it is at right angles to the blade (Fig.233). This, plus their rugged construction, differentiates them from the bow saw (Fig.234)(which is used more in the vertical position, and has two handles, both parallel to the blade.)

Fig.232   Ice saw. The handle on the top left, when attached, extends almost parallel to the blade.

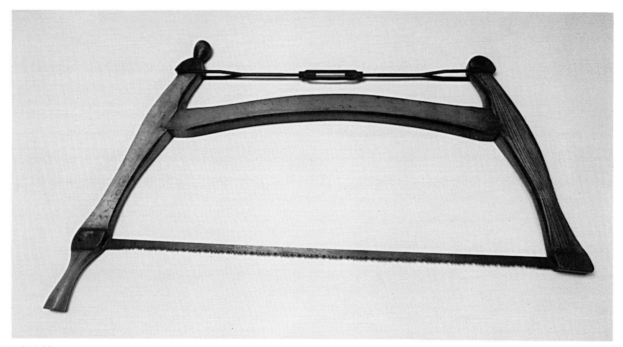

Fig.233   Buck saw.

BOW SAW

Ranging from a blade of 6" to 36" these saws were used mostly for curved work by carpenters and coopers. The tension on the blade was created by twisting the string at the top by means of a tightening or "toggle" stick (Fig.234). Sometimes a threaded rod and wingnut were used in place of the string. There are some elaborate models made from exotic woods that are most attractive and more valuable.

The bow saw has a few characteristics that might concern the collector in judging the authenticity of the parts:

1. If both handles are not the same length, it doesn't necessarily mean they are wrong. More often than not, they were originally made that way, as the bottom, or "power" handle, required more length for better gripping. Just be sure the design and type wood are the same for both. Most handles were made of beech or fruitwood, with the better ones of boxwood.

2. The toggle stick is generally not original; in some cases it is missing altogether. Although any replaced part detracts from value, this is one case where it is minimal.

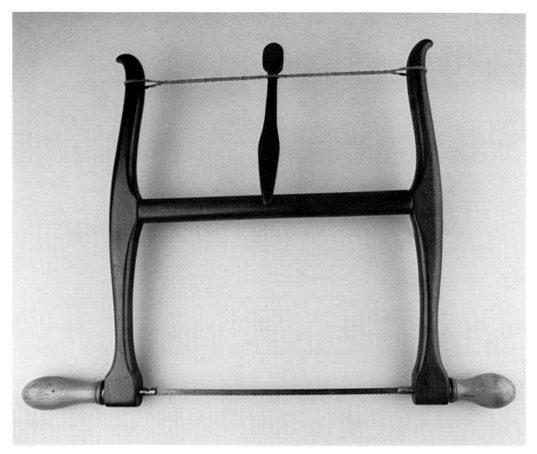

Fig.234 Bow saw tightened with toggle stick.

TURNING or FELLOE SAW

Turning saws were used by wheelwrights to cut felloes (sections of the wheel), chairmakers to cut seats, and carpenters for large curved sections of millwork. These framed saws ranged up to 40" and were put together with tight mortise and tenon joints. Many have artistically forged "rams horn" nuts to apply tension to the blade (Fig.235), which add to the tool's appeal.

STAIR SAW

Stair saws are both home-made and factory-made, with the former producing the more interesting shapes (Fig.236). This saw cuts the grooves in the staircase frame (stringer) that the treads and risers fit into.

Fig.235   *Turning or felloe saw.*

Fig.236   *Two home made stair saws.*

ONE-MAN ONE-HANDED SAWS

HAND SAW

The most common of all saws used today (without power) is the hand saw. Although many other type saws are used with one hand, the name hand saw is generally reserved for the familiar rip or cross-cut saw that can be found in any carpenter's box (Fig.237). The ornate handles used around the turn of the century have been replaced with modern plainer ones, and very little of the picturesque engraving on the blade is done any longer. But what has really been lost is the fit and feel of the saw. The older saw handles seem almost molded from a human hand. They feel good! Not so with the ones purchased today. Perhaps the heavy dependency on power saws has relegated the hand saw to infrequent usage, and things like fit and feel are no longer important.

The two major types of hand saws are rip (cutting with the grain) and cross-cut (cutting against the grain). The difference in the shape of the teeth was previously explained. Hand saws are designated by so many "points" per inch. Interesting is the manner in which these points are counted. The count is made over one inch, starting at the tip of the first tooth and counting all teeth tips (or "points") up to *and including* the last one at the end of the inch mark. This is not an accurate measure of teeth per inch, as a 10 point saw doesn't have 10 full teeth per inch (it only has 9). But it does have 10 *points* per inch, and that is what the sawmaker is claiming.

Fig.237   Hand saws. The bottom saw is an earlier example with a nib near the top end. Controversy exists as to the purpose of the nib; old woodworkers offer varying theories: simply decorative, a place on which to tie the saw guard, or a projection to mark and start the cut.

BACK SAW: DOVETAIL, TENON, or MITER

These saws (Fig.238) vary in size from the small dovetail saw used to cut the dovetail joint in chests and furniture (1" to 2" wide), through the tenon saw used for cutting the tenon portion of the mortise and tenon joint (approximately 3" wide), up to the miter saw used in conjunction with the miter box (Fig.239) for cutting boards and molding on an angle (up to 6" wide). The miter and tenon saws have closed handles, while the dovetail saw has an open handle, usually parallel to the blade. Two features shared by all three types is the near rectangular blade shape, and the stiffening strip on the back side (opposite the teeth). Although most back saws have steel stiffening strips, many of the English- made models have brass strips, giving the saw a better look.

Fig.238   *Back saws. From top to bottom: miter, tenon, large dovetail, small dovetail.*

Fig.239   *Miter box with saw in cutting position.*

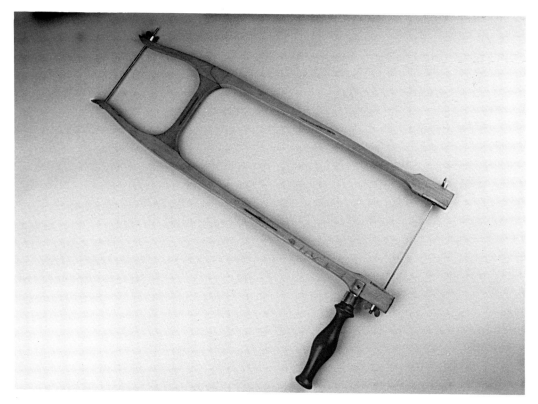

Fig.240   *Fret saw made by the Sorrento Wood Carving Co. and patented Dec.13,1870.*

FRET or COPING SAW

Because of its thin narrow blade, this saw can cut very small arcs and is used in marquetry (inlay work). Its deep throat allows for greater turning clearances and therefore larger panels. The patented model in Fig.240 is made of a maple frame with a rosewood handle. A version of this saw, originating in the United States, the coping saw, is used for small trim work on moldings and other fine curves.

COMPASS SAW

This narrow tapered saw with an average 12" blade is used mostly for making internal cutouts, particularly larger circles. It has an open handle (Fig.241).

Fig.241 *Early compass saw.*

PAD or KEYHOLE SAW

The pad saw is smaller than the compass saw, with most blades only ½" at the widest point. The blade fits into a slotted handle made of beech, boxwood, rosewood or ebony (Fig.242). It is used for very small cutout work, hence the name keyhole.

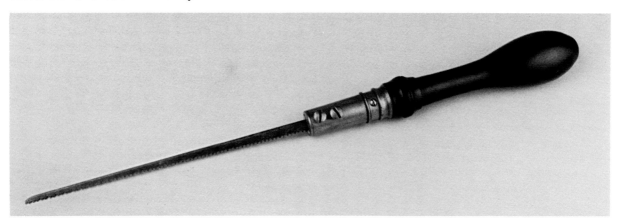

Fig.242 *Pad or keyhole saw.*

JEWELER'S SAW

Perhaps the most demanding and delicate of all saw work is done with the jeweler's saw. Used mostly on metal, it is also used for very fine work in ivory and wood (Fig.243).

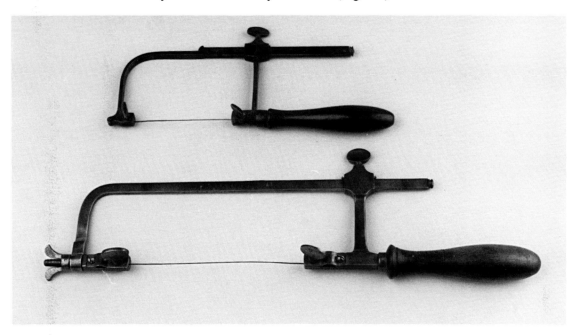

Fig.243 *Jeweler's saws.*

HACK SAW

A metal cutting saw used both in machine shops and wood shops (Fig.244). Many were blacksmith-made.

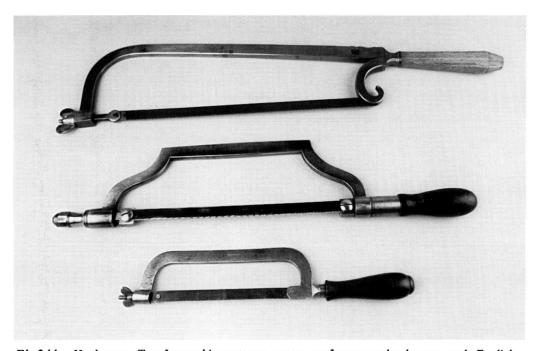

Fig.244 *Hack saws. Top, Lancashire pattern; center, craftsman-made; bottom, early English-made by Stubs.*

SAWSETS

The sawset (Fig.245) is used to bend the tooth outward to provide clearance for the blade in the cut. There are almost as many varieties of sawsets as there are mousetraps, each creator thinking his was slightly better. However there are three classic styles that did survive: the comb type (or wrest), which fits over the tooth and bends it directly; the pliers type that levers the tooth over; and the hammer type, where the larger teeth are hammered over. Some collectors maintain that if you come across a tool that you can't identify at all, it is probably a sawset.

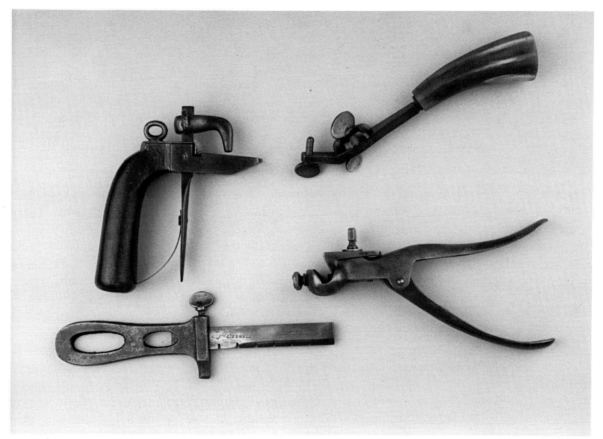

Fig.245 *Sawsets. Top left, O.K. brand patented Feb. 13, 1866; bottom left, marked patent pending; top right, a Stillman patent, 1848, with horn handle; bottom right, Morrill's patent.*

OTHER TOOLS

This chapter describes many of the tools not discussed under the previous headings. Here we will cover taps and screwboxes, hammers and mallets, clamps and vises, screwdrivers, wrenches, and tool chests. These generally attract less interest, although some of the most avid tool collectors are the wrench and hammer enthusiasts; and some of the most breathtaking pieces are tool chests. True, there are still a few categories omitted - scissors, awls, files, sharpening stones, anvils, etc. - but these and others you may wish to learn about can be found in more detailed works such as Salaman's *Dictionary of Tools* (see Books to Read).

TAPS AND SCREWBOXES

Before the standardization of threads during the industrial revolution, most taps were made by the local blacksmith specifically for the woodworker. Exact size and pitch (number of threads per inch) did not matter, as the woodworker would make his matching screwbox from the tap. Obviously, they were only good in pairs, and a matched tap and screwbox is worth considerably more today than an unmatched pair. And if they can still cut threads (evidenced by sharp-edged cutting surfaces), they are worth even more (Fig.246).

The tap is a non-adjustable tool that cuts a specific size internal thread. Most taps have the forward end of their cutting flutes tapered to make for an easier start. Some taps are tapered the entire distance of the cutters, so as to slowly enlarge the thread to its full depth. Tapping through "flat- grain" (perpendicular to the upright direction of the tree) is the easiest way to use a tap. If it has to be used through the "end-grain" (straight up the tree), a more suitable tap is generally used. This type is hollow throughout, with a small perpendicular hole through the starting thread. The smaller hole has a v-shaped razor edge that actually does all the cutting.

Screwboxes (called dies in metalwork) are more complicated than taps. A single v-shaped cutter is positioned to take the depth of cut in one pass. Where more than one pass is desired, the cutter has to be reset each time. The dowel to be cut is inserted into the plain hole end of the screwbox and turned past the cutter. As the thread is cut, it exits the box by passing through the matching female threads. The female threads provide a guide for the proper spacing of the remaining male threads to be cut.

When the screwbox has no handles, it is generally held in a vise, and the dowel is turned through it. Larger screwboxes normally have handles and the dowel is held in the vise or sometimes in a lathe. Taps and screwboxes had many uses: screw arms for plow planes and wooden clamps and vises are just a few examples.

To sharpen or set the v-shaped cutting tool, the screwbox is taken apart. If you intend to take the box apart for curiousity or restoration, be sure you remember the proper position of the cutter. And be careful not to lose any of the shims that are used to give the cutter a tight fit.

Fig.246   Screw box and tap.

HAMMERS AND MALLETS

We would suppose that the hammer (in the form of a stone) was among man's first tools, and it has not changed that much over the years. From the cast head of the Bronze Age, it evolved to added "claws" in the Roman era. The biggest change the hammer has seen in recent times is the one-piece model. This all-steel hammer, in which the head and the handle are combined, is modern industry's answer to the biggest problems the hammer faces - broken and loose handles. But even so, most carpenters prefer the hickory handles for weight and feel. The most common types the collector will find are pictured below.

Fig.247   Claw hammers. Above, a framing hammer. Below, a Roman style.

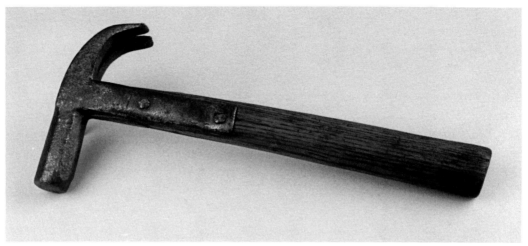

Fig.248   *Strapped eye hammer. Found as early as the 16th century. It has the advantage of added strength at the junction of the head and the handle.*

Fig.249   *Two ball peen machinist's hammers. The one below has a "PERFECT" type wood-filled handle.*

Fig.250   *Tinsmith's or tin knocker's hammer. Used to form sheet metal or to knock out dents.*

Fig.251 *Upholsterer's hammers. Above a strapped-eye variety. Below an English example, ca.1700.*

Fig.252 *Blacksmith's hammers. Several shapes used to form the red hot iron: on the left, a top fuller for grooves; center, a top swage for rounding; on the right, a punch for holes. These hammers are not swung, but are struck with another hammer.*

Fig.253 *Cobbler's hammers, used by shoemakers. Upper, German pattern; lower, French pattern.*

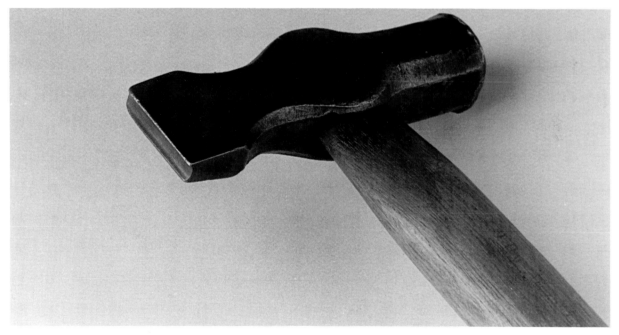

Fig.254 *Cooper's hammer. Used for driving the hoop down over the barrel. The notched end fits over the hoop and the head end is then struck with another hammer.*

Fig.255 *Double claw hammer. Rare. Used to get better leverage on long nails. This tool is sometimes faked with modern welding techniques. Beware of highly polished heads (sometimes done to hide the acetylene weld between the two sets of claws.*

Fig.256 *Crating hammer. More of a combination tool: hammer, hatchet, pry, and nail remover. Used to open wooden boxes*

Fig.257 *Slater's hammers. Used to install slate roofing shingles.*

Fig.258 *Bricklayer's hammer. Used to size the bricks (when shorter sizes are needed) and also to tap the bricks square and level.*

Fig.259 *Marking hammer. The face of this hammer has letters, numbers, or a logo for identifying lumber or trees.*

Fig.260 *Above, farrier's hammer, for driving and clinching the nails in horseshoes. Below, saddlemaker's hammer.*

Fig.261 *"Saw doctor's" hammers, for adjusting tension into the saw blade and flattening or leveling large circular saw blades.*

Fig.262 *Veneer hammers, used to press the glued veneer into position and remove air pockets and lumps.*

Fig.263 *Left, a carpenter's mallet, a standard working mallet. Right, a carver's mallet, for striking chisels; the round head is quite often made of lignum vitae (a very heavy and hard wood).*

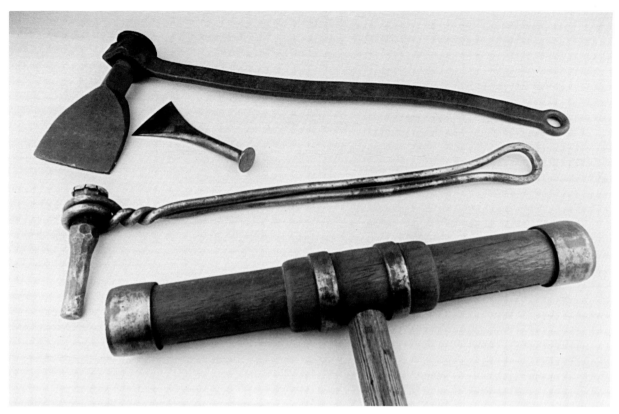

Fig.264 *At bottom, a caulking mallet. Above, caulking irons used to drive the caulking material into the ship's seams. The one on top is called a hawsing iron.*

Fig.265 *Wheelwright's mallet. Used by wheelwrights (in lieu of the sledge) to drive spokes into the hub. Many short-handled mallets of this style have been found in carpenters' boxes.*

-166-

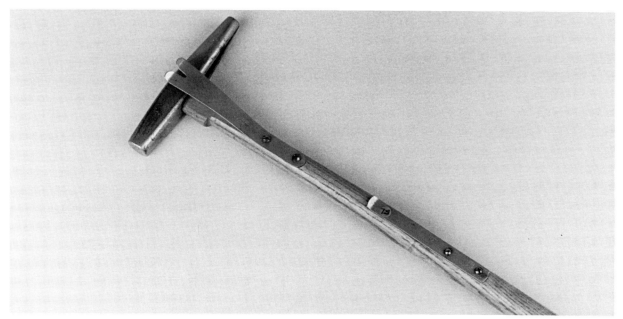

Fig.266 *The A.R. Robertson patent bill posting hammer, that allows for mounting posters beyond arm's reach. The hammer holds the poster and the nail simultaneously. This hammer (patented Nov.2, 1886) was available in a two-section 36" model and a three-section 45" model.*

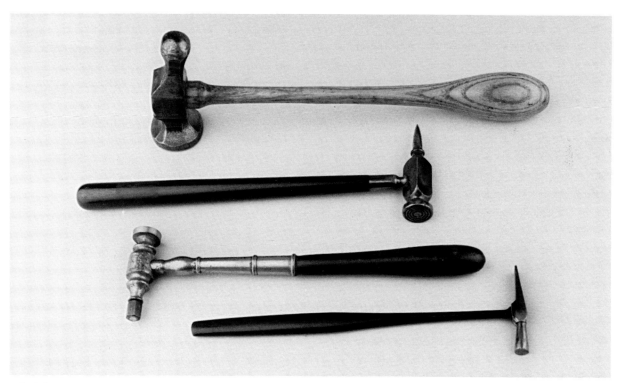

Fig.267 *Jeweler's and silversmith's hammers, used for delicate work. Top, repousse hammer used to shape thin sheets of metal, e.g., copper and silver, into a relief pattern. Center two, jeweler's hammers. Bottom, watchmaker's hammer.*

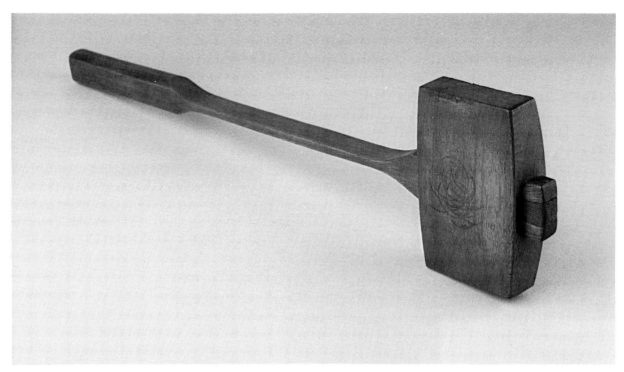

Fig.268 *Bung starter. Used by cellarmen (wine and liquor warehousemen) to "start" (or startle) the bung, by striking the side of the barrel so as to loosen the bung for removal. Also used for sounding the cask to determine fullness.*

Fig.269 *Decorative hammer; probably used in the household. Charles T. Hennig patent, Sept. 17, 1901, Brooklyn, NY.*

CLAMPS AND VISES

In woodworking, as in many other skills, the proper way of holding the work is far more critical than the novice might imagine, particularly during glueing. Clamps (called cramps in England) and vises assure this.

PARALLEL CLAMP (or HAND SCREW)

Generally ranging from 6" to 24" and made from beech, birch, or maple (Fig.270). These general purpose clamps are still used today - although most modern clamps of this type have steel, rather than wooden, screw arms. The first thing to check before buying an old hand screw is whether the screw arms move freely. In many cases they do not, and the buyer must decide whether a little cleanup and some wax is all that is needed or if the screws are "frozen" to the sides. If they appear frozen, check to see that the threads are not broken where the screw arm mates with the side piece. If they are broken, the likelihood of freeing the internal chips is slim, and the piece should be considered as a decorative "wall-hanger." However, if the threads are solid, they are probably swollen together. Penetrating oil (or any kind of oil) will generally not help. Silicon sprays will not reach the source of the problem. The "growth" of the threads more than likely occurred because of moisture over an extended period of time. In many cases, drying out (in the hot sun for a day, or the oven at 120°F. for an hour or so) will allow you to work the arms loose. Once they are free of each other, you can work on cleaning up the threads to allow a smooth action. Sometimes this will require filing. If you get good at this technique, you can try your hand at bound-up plow plane arms, another common malady. Here is where you can significantly increase the value of your antique tool.

Fig.270 Parallel clamps.

FURNITURE CLAMP (BAR or PIPE)

The main wooden bar is usually between 3 feet and 6 feet long (Fig.271). The later type using a pipe for a bar can go up to 10 feet. The name describes its usage: the making of furniture.

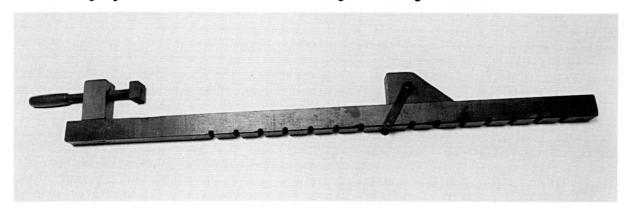

Fig.271 *Furniture clamp.*

C-CLAMP

Almost always made of metal with jaw openings ranging to 16" or more (Fig.272). They have the advantage of strength over wooden clamps. Problems found when buying old c-clamps are bent screws and missing swivels at the end of the screws, either of which greatly reduce the clamp's value.

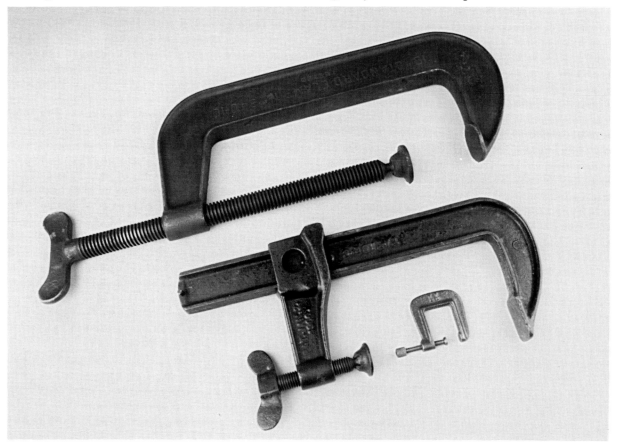

Fig.272 *C-clamps.*

WOODWORKER'S VISE

These vises were built into the workbench. Early vises were made entirely of wood, while later models have metal parts, particularly the screw mechanism. Once again, be sure of a smooth screw action if your intention is to use the tool.

METALWORKER'S VISE

Early handforged models are beautifully crafted, sometimes with elaborate chamfering. Later cast models range upwards in size and many have anvil-like platforms integral to the rear of the vise (Figs.273 and 274).

Fig.273   Early blacksmith-made metalworker's bench vise.

Fig.274   Some manufactured metalworker's bench vises.

BLACKSMITH'S or LEG VISE

Most often handforged, the leg was used to support the vise and absorb the shock during any downward pounding (Fig.275).

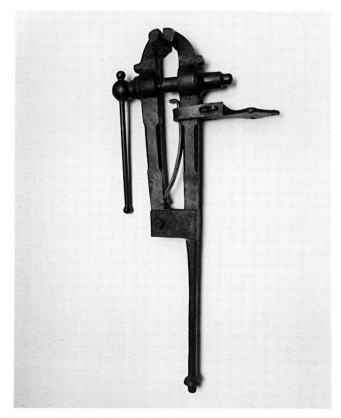

Fig.275   Blacksmith's leg vise.

HAND VISE

As the name implies, these are small vises that are hand held (Fig.276).

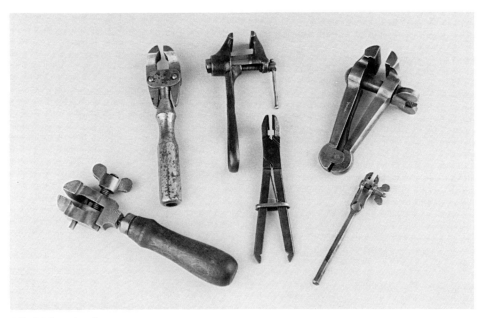

Fig.276   Hand vises.

SAW VISE

Originally of wood, the later factory models were all metal, and operated with a toggle clamp so the blade could be quickly loosened and moved along. These were used to hold the saw blade when sharpening or setting the teeth (Fig.277).

Fig.277 Saw vise.

SCREWDRIVERS

A tool late in coming (18th century), there are only a few major variations, shown below.

Turnscrew, Fig.278.
Perfect Handle Screwdriver, Fig. 279.
Spiral Screwdriver (Yankee type), Fig.279.
Patented Model, Fig.279.

The age of a tool can sometimes be approximated by the kind of metal screws used on it:

Handmade screws with pointed tips and somewhat irregular threads	late 18th c.
Machine made screws with flattened tips	early to mid 19th c.
Machine made screws with pointed tips	mid 19th c. and later.
Brass screws	late 19th c. and later.
Phillips head screws (with cross slots)	mid 20th c. and later.

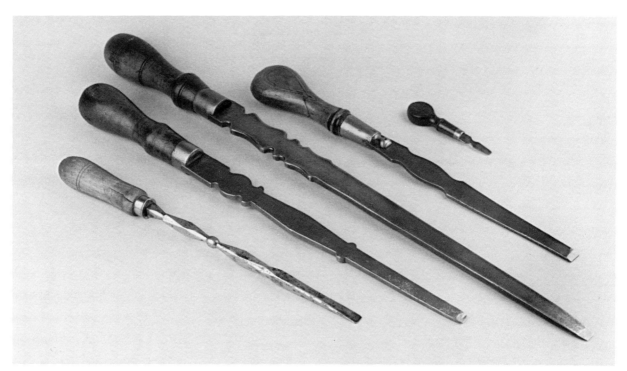

Fig.278 *Turnscrews.*

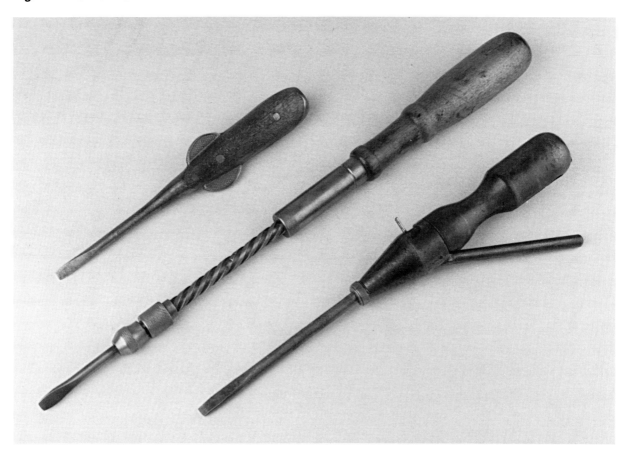

Fig.279 *Screwdrivers. From the left: Perfect handle, spiral, and a patented variety.*

WRENCHES

Wrenches are also latecomers in the tool world, not needed until threaded nuts and bolts were made. However, there is an enormous variety of standard and patent models, which makes collecting them most interesting.

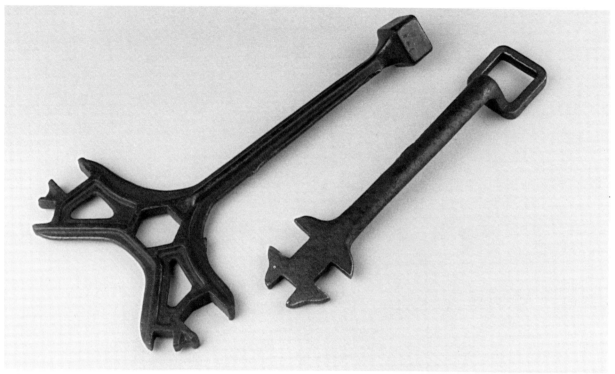

Fig.280   Combination open end and box wrenches.

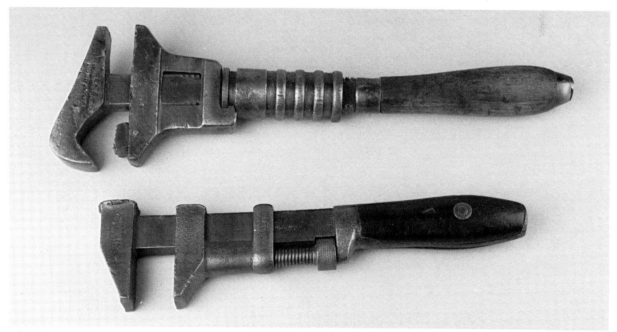

Fig.281   Below, a monkey wrench; above, a combination monkey and pipe wrench.

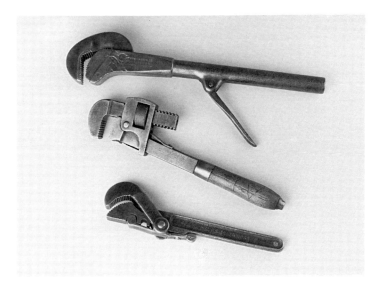

Fig.282   *Pipe wrenches.*

Fig.283   *Alligator wrenches.*

Fig.284   *Twisted handle wrenches.*

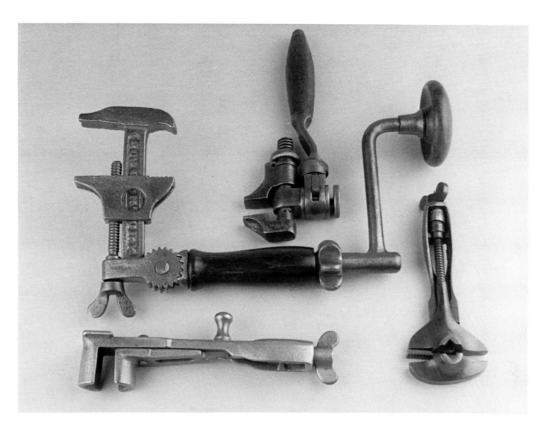

Fig.285 *Buggy wrenches*

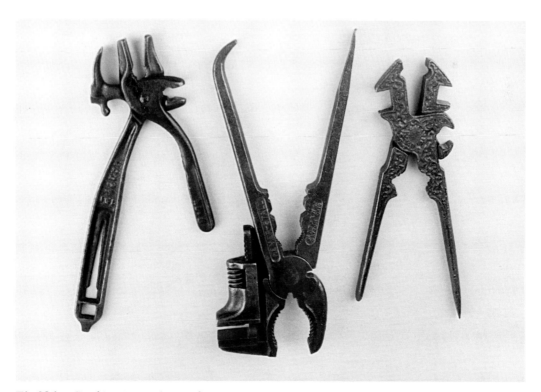

Fig.286 *Combination tool wrenches.*

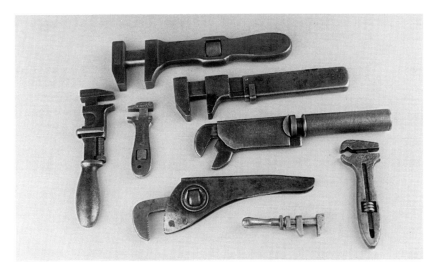

Fig.287   *Billings and similar type wrenches.*

Fig.288   *Double headed wrench and other types.*

Fig.289   *A few more of the endless variety of wrench patents.*

TOOL CHESTS

Besides needing a place to keep his tools, the cabinetmaker of the 19th century often wanted a display piece to show off his skills. The dovetailed, multi-drawered, inlaid tool chest was perfect for this. The master woodworker would sometimes have his apprentice work on one of these boxes throughout his apprenticeship, and have him take it with him upon "graduation." It was both a present and a start in his new career. In the more elaborate boxes, five or six drawers are contained in one section called a till, which slides or rolls across the box to allow access to other areas. Some chests have as many as four tills. In addition, there are saw racks, plane compartments and hidden compartments. Although the outside of these boxes are usually unimpressive, the inside rivals the most magnificent furniture, with its panelling, marquetry and veneer work (Fig.290).

Such a tool chest is often the centerpiece of a collection and represents the very core of woodworking. It is a fitting piece with which to end our description of tools.

Fig.290   Tool chest.

MATERIALS USED IN TOOLS

WOOD

It takes both knowledge and experience to be able to identify the different wood species used for tools. There are books on the subject and also wood sample kits available from wood supply companies. Whichever way you decide to pursue the subject, it's helpful to have an experienced person label examples for you, perhaps using some of the tools you've already collected, pointing out the distinguishing features of each species. Meanwhile, let's see if we can provide some insights.

APPLE	Pinkish-brown, smooth textured. Used for tool handles, planes and braces.
BEECH	Light to dark brown with telltale ray lines and flecks. Used for planes, braces, and almost all tools.
BIRCH	Orangey-brown with many tiny darkened pores. Used for planes and braces — mostly in New England.
BOXWOOD	Straw to brown, tight closely textured grain. Used for rules, wear strips on molding planes and handles.
CORMIER	Pinkish-brown, looking like our apple but softer. Used mostly by the French for planes and routers.
CHERRY	Redder and grainier than apple. Used for levels and handles.
EBONY	Jet black to brownish-black. Almost plastic looking. Used for handles, gauges, small levels, infill of English tools.
HICKORY	Medium brown, long streaky grain. Used for impact handles and frame saws.
HORNBEAM	Yellowish-brown mottled look with flecks. Used on the European continent for planes, braces, and routers.
LIGNUM VITAE	Dark brown with yellow striations, sometimes including the light colored sapwood. Used for brace heads, mallet heads, wear strips, and ship's planes.
MAHOGANY	Medium reddish-brown; nice grainy look. Used for levels, infills of English tools and handles.
MAPLE	Sandy brown bland looking, except for the "tiger" variety. Used for tool handles, some measuring tools, homemade planes, and braces.
OAK	Medium brown with heavily pronounced rays. Mostly used in homemade tools.
ROSEWOOD	Dark reddish-brown with black striations. Wavy and dramatic multi-colored grain. Used for handles, levels, measuring instruments, and infill of English tools.

Fig.291 Types of wood used for tools. We have tried to list those woods most often used for tools and their most common characteristics. There are, however, so many variations within each species that the general description in this chart will not pertain in all cases. But it is a good place to start.

Wood identification is easier in the classroom with fresh clean samples (Fig.291). In real life, particularly in tool collecting, the piece is most likely covered with a patina from long use or possibly just grime. Also it is unlikely that you'll be able to cut a sliver for a cross section analysis under high magnification. However, there are some basic rules that will help, even under adverse conditions.

The wood most commonly used for tools is beech. Though it is a distant cousin to birch and maple, the three are not easy to tell apart. They are light-toned woods, but can patina to almost a walnut hue. Maple, used occasionally for handles and braces, is rarely used for planes (except homemade ones), so the choice for molding planes is almost always birch or beech. Early American planemakers, particularly those in 18th century New England used a lot of birch, but wooden planes made after 1800 were most often beech. Some woods are known as tight-grained woods. That means it's difficult to see the pores in either cross section or longitudinal section. These pores represent the cellular structure of the faster growing wood (which occurs in the spring). As they only occur once a year, they are known as annual rings and are used to determine the tree's age (Fig.292).

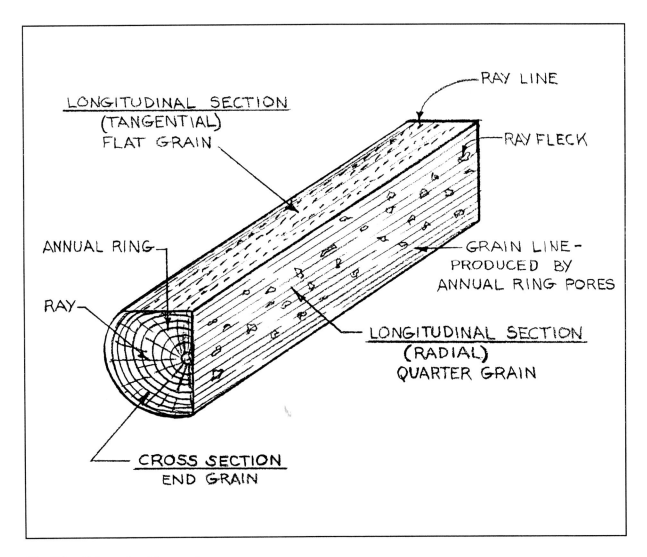

Fig.292   Schematic of log sections.

There are degrees of this so-called tightness of grain. Boxwood, one of the lightest colored tool woods (straw yellow), has such tight grain that it looks almost homogeneous throughout. This tight grain and its resistance to wear made it desirable for the "boxing" or wear strips in molding planes. Hard maple and applewood are both considered tight grained, but they can be differentiated by their difference in color. Hard maple is a light sandy color, while apple is a light pinkish brown. Yellow birch and beech are more open-grained than the above species. Both are light brown, but birch has a more orangy hue. Birch has many, many tiny linear openings (pores) that are usually darkened with grime. They can be seen on the longitudinal sections (top and sides of the plane). Beech has a characteristic that will help considerably in its identification, pronounced rays that can be seen as tiny lines or light flecks (Fig.292). Don't confuse the many dark-toned dash-type markings in birch with the many tiny ray lines or flecks in beech. The rays in beech are solid material, while the birch openings are just that — openings. A magnifying glass will help.

Cherry and apple were the fruitwoods most often used. Cherry has a reddish hue to its brown color, and although it looks very much like apple, it is grainier, i.e., more lines and pores show. Another characteristic of cherry, often used for decorative effect, is the contrast in color between the sapwood (outerwood next to the bark) and the heartwood (innerwood circling the core). The sapwood is almost white. Many woodworkers used the sapwood and the heartwood in the same piece — for effect.

The woods in the next group are not botanical "cousins," but all are dark in color. Ebony can be either jet black (Ceylon ebony) or have dark brownish streaks or hues (Macassar ebony). But you'll know it's ebony because of its extremely smooth surface. Ebony is also very heavy; it sinks in water.

Rosewood shows color striations that range from reddish brown to almost black. There are many species of rosewood, the most common used in tools being East India rosewood, which is darker and more solid in color. Another species, Brazilian rosewood, was used starting in the late 19th century. It is more orangey in hue and dramatic in grain figuring. Lignum vitae (another wood that sinks) also has striations resembling rosewood but varies (in the same piece of wood) between brown and yellow and, unlike rosewood, is very tight- grained.

Last in this category are the mahoganys, generally moderately dark brown, with occasional reddish hues, often highly figured and moderately open-grained. They range from moderately heavy to very heavy in weight. There are so many species of mahogany, which grow in South and Central America and Africa that only an expert can tell them apart. Mahogany was most commonly used for levels, for infill in English planes, and for measuring instruments. Although you may find some color striations in the grain, it will not approach the differentiation or contrast of the rosewoods and that's one of the best ways to tell them apart.

Handles that need to absorb shock (e.g., those on axes and adzes) are generally made of hickory, a tough, twisty, open-grained medium brown wood. You will be able to see long grain lines in hickory. Oak, rarely used for tools (except homemade ones) is an extremely open-grained wood with heavy ray flecks.

Hornbeam is a European wood used by German and Austrian toolmakers. It is a light colored, heavily flecked wood. French cormier is a softer wood similar to our apple. Both are common in planes and braces that originate in those countries.

METAL

The iron used for early tools was either forged by blacksmiths from bar stock, or cast into molds at foundries. Casting is used where an ornate pattern does not lend itself to forging. However, cast iron is quite brittle. Consequently we find many cast parts that are cracked or completely broken away.

Steel is a comparatively new metal. In the early 19th century it was relatively expensive to produce, and it was therefore more economical to use a small piece of steel "layed-on" (forged) to the iron for a cutting edge. This line of demarcation between the steel and the iron tends to be a date indicator. As technology progressed into the 20th century, it became more economical to machine forge the entire axe head or plane blade of steel and the use of layed-on steel over iron disappeared. It's not easy to tell steel from iron unless they are side by side, as they are on the older axe heads and plane blades. Iron, particularly cast iron, is more porous, rougher looking and darker. Steel doesn't pit as badly as iron and maintains a smoother look. From a metallurgical standpoint, steel is an alloy of iron, with controlled amounts of carbon for hardness and other metals for strength.

Other metals used for tools were basically copper alloys. Pure copper was rarely used, except occasionally for ferrules. The copper alloys were:

Brass — copper and zinc — it has a golden yellow hue.
Bronze — copper and tin — orangey with a slight pinkish hue.
Gun metal — copper and tin with some zinc —looks (and is) very much like bronze.
German silver — copper, zinc and nickel —(note: although rarely with any silver content, it is silvery looking). Its use in tools was mainly decorative.

As iron tends to rust and brass turns dark, a final finish or coating was often applied. With brass it could be an electro- plate, using mostly tin. In other cases, such as the strengthening plates on Sheffield braces, the brass was merely coated with a lacquer. Occasionally we find brass tools with their finish in the original condition, which tends to increase value. More often, however, the overcoating is either partially or completely worn off. Iron was frequently either japanned (coated with lacquer or varnish compound - usually black - and baked), or nickel plated. Most of the early Stanley tools were japanned; later models were nickel plated.

IVORY, BONE AND HORN

These materials were used only occasionally in tools. Bone and horn were used most often for handles, with one valuable exception — the very rare horn-filled Ultimatum brace.

Ivory was used primarily in premium quality rules, bow drill spindles, and as a decorative feature in the highest quality planes and braces. Tools with ivory parts are more valuable than the more basic types.

We are often asked "How can I tell ivory from bone?" If it's a factory made rule, you can assume it's ivory. Otherwise you'll have to look for grain. Ivory has growth rings similar to those in wood, and produces a very fine grain effect. Bone is considerably more striated in tone and grain, and slightly darker in color. Ivory does fade and "yellow" as can be seen on the outside folds of many rules. It's almost impossible to remove this yellowing. It's best just to lightly clean away the surface grime and forget it, or you'll take what is left of the numbers off trying to remove the yellow.

Ivory parts have been replaced throughout the years when the originals have been lost, e.g. rings in the heads of braces and the tips of plane fence arms. The slight checking and yellowing that is produced in aged ivory is generally not seen in the replaced parts. Some collectors express concern about replaced ivory. We feel that if the part was orginally ivory and is properly replaced, that's acceptable maintenance. But if the ivory is added to a piece that was never orginally made that way, that's misrepresentation. Many ivory-tipped plow planes made by Sandusky, Ohio Tool Co., and others carry their style numbers stamped on the plane and this will help to verify their authenticity.

Understanding the materials used is basic to collecting and to any restoration work you may undertake. The time spent learning these basics will increase your pleasure and effectiveness as a collector.

CLEANING, RESTORING, AND DISPLAYING TOOLS

There is no issue among tool collectors that has caused as much controversy as cleaning and restoring. The battle lines are generally drawn between the "purists" and the "realists," i.e. those wishing to preserve the tool in its *as-found* condition, and those wishing to bring the piece up to its functional usage or *as-used* condition. Although we tend to favor the latter, we respect both views and certainly do not propose indiscriminate restoration or cleaning. We believe that if possible a tool should be restored to the same condition it would have had when owned and used by a skilled and caring craftsman.

An interesting example of this issue is the case of a molding plane with a missing wedge. If a proper wedge profile can be taken from a complete and original plane, if the correct wood is used, if the patina is matched, and if the restorer's initials (or the date) is stamped into the hidden part of the wedge, we feel the plane has become a more useful and satisfying part of a collection. The argument offered against this is that you can never be positive that the wedge profile selected is absolutely correct. We will briefly outline those techniques for cleaning, preserving, and restoring that the collector may, if he wishes, choose to follow.

CLEANING

Cleaning procedures differ in their degrees of severity, ranging from soap and water all the way to strippers on wood; and from fine steel wood to sand blasting on metal. We would like to offer one criterion for cleaning wood *or* metal: the tool should be no cleaner, nor any dirtier, than it would have been when on a caring workman's bench when it was originally used. This means that while red rust or flaking corrosion on iron parts would not be acceptable, a gray oxidation would be normal. Bringing these parts up to a high polish is foreign to what the part ever looked like during its working lifetime, and should be avoided.

There will be times when the piece has been allowed to become so dirty and rusty that strippers and wirewheels are the only answer. Here is where skill is needed to prevent irreversible damage. In a short chapter we can't teach skill. Only practice will do that. We will, however, give you a variety of methods that you can try.

CLEANING WOOD

Soap and Water takes off surface grime but is not really good enough in most cases. It also tends to raise the grain of the wood.

Household Cleaners are not bad, but are not effective with paint, tar and the like.

Linseed Oil and Turpentine mixture is popular, as it has both a cleaning and a preserving agent. Some people are opposed to the smell and the residue.

Strippers (liquid or paste) remove almost all problems except deep staining, but in many cases will also remove the patina. The patina is the surface change of the material brought on by years of oxidation and usage. It is natural to the piece and when it is removed, a "naked" look is created. Expert restorers can duplicate this patina, but most beginners cannot. We feel that the piece is better dirty than naked, so if you can't get the patina back, don't take it off! You might experiment with partial removal by paste strippers: the stripper is applied with steel wool and rubbed immediately upon contact. This may sound as if it won't work, because most stripper directions tell you to wait 20 minutes or so before trying to remove the finish. However it works fine if you have a sensitive touch and just want to break through the outer grime. A good general rule is to test whatever you do on a small sample first and, when committed, to work gently and gradually. And always follow the safety instructions.

CLEANING METAL

Brass and bronze can be cleaned with brass cleaners from the hardware store if the oxidation is not very heavy. If the crust is deep, industrial cleaners (heavier in acid content) can be used to quicken the job. Precaution must be taken with these cleaners, which require gloves, masks, face shields and proper ventilation. Rag wheels with cutting compounds such as tripoli or rouge will also remove oxidation but might bring the luster up too high. If the wheels are available, and the collector has the skill to use them, an undesirable luster can be killed with liquid cleaners. The biggest problem with liquid cleaners is they tend to get *everything* clean, even the recesses. These areas would not normally be clean in the life of the tool, and if every nook and cranny is sparkling, a very unnatural, naked look results.

Iron or steel can be wire-wheeled if a fine enough wheel is used. Experiment with wheels that do not take off more than you want. Remember, the difference in the hardness of the steel will give you a difference in results with the same wheel. If the wheel is not coarse enough, it will merely burnish the rust into the surface and you will defeat your purpose. (Some wheels are so fine, they will hardly break your own skin.) If the surface is exceedingly rusty, you might start off with emery paper, or use an old knife blade to loosen rust spots, until you're down to where wire wheels can be used. This takes sensitivity and skill — if you break through the patina and leave a shiny spot, you're in trouble. It's possible to acid etch the spot back to gray again, but this is not desirable.

We do not recommend sand or glass blasting, or using chemicals such as "naval jelly." All the natural life of the piece is destroyed with these techniques.

PRESERVING

PRESERVING WOOD

Linseed Oil (the boiled kind) rubbed in with rag or hand is fine in most cases. It's easy and it does some good. There is some objection to its shallow penetration, and some claim that it may raise the grain.

Tung Oil is better for penetration and it dries hard. Be sure to follow the instructions to avoid stickiness.

Wax is easy to apply and can be buffed to any degree of luster. The penetration is not as good as oil, however.

French Polish, a commercial mixture of lacquer and other finishes, gives the benefits of both oil and wax, but takes skill to apply.

PRESERVING METAL

A light machine or mineral oil is best, but some prefer wax, french polish, or a rubbing lacquer. The last two are used on brass more than on iron or steel.

RESTORING

RESTORING WOOD

Missing wood can be replaced only by a skilled woodworker. A botched repair is worse than no repair. However, small holes, chips, or cracks can be filled with a variety of fillers from the hardware store. Many come already stained; they are better to use. Although most of the "plastic wood" types are difficult to stain after hardening, they can easily be stained when the filler is partially dry.

Staining is a "feel" operation. It is mix and try. Penetrants such as the aniline dyes are quick drying but harder to work with in large areas, and have a fading problem in bright sunlight. The oil stains are better for those who have the patience to wait for them to dry.

If you can, try to keep from sanding the wood. If you must do so because of matching to a new piece, steel wool after sanding and then burnish to get the surface fibers to lay down. "Feather" the sanding, i.e., gradually sand outward from the affected area to prevent a noticeable perimeter. When you stain to match, you will have to do the same thing.

RESTORING METAL

Unless you have some machining capabilities, or are willing to pay machine shop rates, you probably won't become involved in making metal parts. Some pieces can be made with a hacksaw and a file, but unless you are a craftsman, that's exactly what they will look like. If you can make a new metal part, you'll have to get rid of that new look. Many solutions are available in paint stores and gun stores that will do this.

We will not get into the caveats of working with metal because of the complexity of the subject. There are many books that will give you the rudiments of machining, blacksmithing and heat treating, if you wish to try some at home. There are, however, a few simple warnings worth mentioning. Cast iron parts usually break under shock (such as dropping on concrete). If you are lucky enough to find only a bent section of a cast iron part, *don't try to straighten it.* Even experts have difficulty with that. An area that you can do some good with is bent screws. If they are old and corroded, you'd be wiser to try to get them back as-is (if you choose not to replace them). But if they have enough life left, heat them up to cherry-red before restraightening. They are far less likely to snap from "fatigue" if you do this.

Collectors find that the easiest way to replace a missing part is to take one from a tool that is similar but in a worthless condition. There are a few warnings here. If the replaced part is from a model of another vintage, you have a bastardized piece. If it's a threaded part and the threads are slightly different (as many of them are), you can easily strip the threads trying to force in the wrong part. Good sense has to be used when cannibalizing. Needless to say, this is a very important point to look for when purchasing pieces that are susceptible to this practice, such as Stanley planes. There is also a question of personal ethics should you decide to trade or sell a piece that has had this type of repair.

DISPLAYING

It is a shame that so many collections rest in cardboard boxes. If there is absolutely no room anywhere, this can't be helped. But a collection can be displayed attractively even in a garage or cellar. The time and small expense necessary to display your collection is well worth it. Aside from the satisfaction gained, you will be in a better position to know what you still need and what you should discard. It will give you an overview of your collection and what direction you might want to pursue. You will avoid the packrat syndrome and have a better opportunity to learn from and enjoy your collection and share it with others. There are a few ways to do this, and they are all fairly obvious.

Tables. Although tables are the easiest way to put out your tools, they don't provide for efficiency of space. Tables can be used for a few of the more spectacular pieces that you wish to "showcase" but beyond that they probably won't do.

Hanging. Most tools can be hung on the wall by using pegboard or paneling. A light background usually shows tools to their best advantage.

Shelves. Planes lend themselves more to shelving than to hanging. Since planes are a major category in many collections, some consideration must be given to shelves. They can go directly on shelf brackets fastened to the studs or cinder block, or can be made independent of the existing wall.

Part of the fun in collecting is acquiring, but displaying for yourself and others can be very rewarding. Don't neglect this aspect of collecting; it's worth it!

BUYING ANTIQUE TOOLS

You will probably acquire most of your antique tools by buying them. It is, therefore, very important to buy wisely, and to do this you must learn to recognize value and know where to find it. Such knowledge comes with experience, but much can also be learned from reading, observing, and talking to dealers and fellow collectors. The purpose of this chapter is to cover the basic information: what factors should determine the price of a tool; where to look for tools; and how to go about buying them.

WHAT DETERMINES THE VALUE OF AN ANTIQUE TOOL

SUPPLY and DEMAND

The most basic of all price determinants is the relationship of supply to demand, the number of buyers versus the supply available for sale, with the price acting as a rationing or auctioning mechanism. Since antique tools are, by definition, finite in number, with no more being made, we have a fixed supply. On the other hand, the number of collectors and the amount of disposable income available to them have been steadily increasing. Therefore, except for the most common tools, prices have been trending higher. This is particularly true of the high end of the market, the classic rarities.

For example, ordinary firmer chisels, draw knives, or mid-19th century wooden jack and fore planes without makers' names have survived in tremendous numbers. They are inexpensive and likely to remain so. At the other extreme, such tools as 18th century crown molders imprinted with their makers' names, Pilkington braces, and pin wheel log calipers are very rare, much sought after, and therefore very expensive. In between are a tremendous variety of interesting tools still available at reasonable, but rising, prices.

Interestingly, some tools that are not nearly so rare as others command a much higher price, so there are other factors at work besides supply and demand. Some of these are:

REGIONAL PREFERENCES

There is often a tendency to collect tools from one's own geographic region. Partly chauvinistic, it is also based on the practical fact that early tools are more often found in the area in which they were made and therefore are more readily available, as is information about them. At any rate, there is frequently less appreciation for the rarity of one region's tools in another region. While premium prices may be paid at a New Hampshire auction when two determined local collectors want a tool made by a New Hampshire maker, the same tool might arouse less interest in Pennsylvania. This tendency is changing, but it is still a reality of the marketplace.

AESTHETIC APPEAL

Some tools have particular appeal because of the materials used, their pleasing forms and proportions, or the high quality of their workmanship. Examples would include many measuring devices, ultimatum braces, rosewood or boxwood plow planes, to name just a very few. Primitive tools may also have some of these qualities.

TOOL SIZE

Closely related to aesthetic appeal is the size of the tool. A seven foot long open pit saw, while relatively rare, presents logistical and display problems. A well-used blacksmith's leg vise, or a furniture clamp, may not fit into the household decor, certainly not as nicely as a plow plane, a delicate bow saw, or an ivory rule.

CONDITION

Condition affects price, sometimes dramatically. A moderately rare Stanley plane, in mint condition and in its original box, will sell for several times that of one in good condition. So will a wooden molding plane with its original patina, a proper wedge and iron, and a crisp maker's mark sell for much more than an example lacking all these qualities.

Sometimes the factors determining condition are specific and unarguable, such as missing parts or damage. Often the judgment is subjective, particularly when the various factors determining condition have to be judged and weighed as to their relative importance to arrive at an over-all valuation.

In the previous chapters, we've pointed out a number of "problems" to watch for. These include:

- A weak, overstruck, or partial maker imprint, which can significantly reduce the value of a tool, particularly where the imprint is the major attraction in an otherwise undistinguished piece.
- Worm holes: a few are usually acceptable; a great many are not.
- Dry rot: often not fully visible, it can render a tool virtually valueless.
- Missing, broken, or improperly replaced parts.
- Cracks in metal tools, hairline or otherwise.
- Bad stains, heavy checking, stripped or damaged threads, molding plane profiles that have been recut.

The condition guide shown below was developed by the *Fine Tool Journal* (Iron Horse Antiques) and is used by some dealers and auctioneers for guidance, particularly in grading metal hand tools, such as planes. It may be helpful to you as a check list.

CATEGORY	USEABLE	FINISH	WEAR	REPAIR	RUST	MISC.
New	totally	100%	none	none	none	+ orig. pkg.
Fine	totally	90-100%	minimal	none	trace	
Good+	yes	75-90%	normal	minor or none	light	some dings or scratch OK
Good	yes	50-75%	norm.-mod.	minor	light	minor chips
Good -	probably	30-50%	mod.-hvy.	correct	mod.	chips OK
Fair	no	0-30%	excessive	major	mod.-hvy.	
Poor	no	n/a	excessive	damaged	heavy	

SETS OF TOOLS

Tools that come in sets or as workman's kits, such as a complete matched set of hollow and round planes, or a stair maker's or musical instrument maker's working kit, have a value above that of their constituent parts.

WHERE AND HOW TO BUY ANTIQUE TOOLS

GARAGE and HOME SALES

Garage sale buying takes preparation. You must look carefully in the house sale section of your newspaper for any indications of tools being included in the sale. However, just *tools* are not good enough; the ad must reflect "old" or "antique" tools. Even then, most of these sales will have only rusty wrenches, drills, and hammers from circa 1930. Perhaps one time in ten, your perserverance will pay off with a real gem or two, often at very reasonable prices. It's wise to phone ahead. You won't always get accurate answers, but if you have a choice of sales, at least you'll be more likely to choose the right one. Remember, the good stuff is usually gone in the first hour or so (sometimes the night before), so you're going to have to hustle. You have to like garage-saling, because most often it is not very productive.

FLEA MARKETS

These can be quite exciting, rather like a treasure hunt or like going fishing: getting up before dawn, having breakfast at the diner, and then hurrying off to try to haul in the "big one." The key here is to get to the "fishing hole" before anyone else does. And that "ain't" easy. Many others know which dealers have tools. You'll find a lot of familiar faces hovering around the same dealer, waiting for him to unload his station wagon. Of course, you can go on "upstream" to look for a new hole, and you might just get lucky. But you have to be quick and aggressive at times, and not too fussy about the weather.

At the big flea markets (such as Brimfield, MA; Bouckville, NY; Adamstown, PA) you'll almost always get something. Most of the experienced regulars "fly" through on their first pass, picking up obvious bargains, and then settle down to more detailed inspection on a second pass. Some avoid the rush and deliberately start later to catch dealers who are slower at setting up. A few will pay an early entrance fee that, at some markets, allows them to get in along with the dealers, before the general public. Whatever technique you use, it's almost always a fun day afield.

TOOL DEALERS

This is by far the most comfortable and most efficient way to buy. You'll find few bargains and you should expect to pay the market price. Some shops are pricier than others. Some dealers price an item based on what it cost them; others simply on what the market will bear. We do find, however, that even the high- priced shops have an occasional bargain. In any event, these shops will usually have some fine tools to look at. It's a wonderful way to educate yourself while feasting your eyes.

Almost all dealers will bargain to some degree. But dealers have to make a living, and when you've hit their bottom line, you risk insulting them if you continue to haggle. If the price is still too high for you after the dealer has brought it down to his "best price," thank him and walk away. You want a friend, not an enemy.

Many of the best tool dealers are in "co-op" type shops. Tool club newsletters, antique newspapers, and fellow collectors will tell you where they are.

Some dealers publish tool catalogs. For a few dollars, you can get a list (most with pictures) of several hundred tools for sale. To find out who is currently active, check tool club periodicals.

ANTIQUE SHOWS

These often include tool dealers as well as general dealers who carry tools along with other items. Again, it's a good place to learn. The dealers are generally knowledgeable and friendly. Don't expect bargains, but unusual items do show up. Watch your newspapers for time and place.

TOOL AUCTIONS

Ah — the auction! Nothing equals it for drama, excitement, and pure entertainment. The five or six hundred lots at an auction assures us that there will be something for everyone. Auctions will give you a sense of market prices and will expose you to other collectors and dealers. The auction catalog, and the subsequent "prices realized" list, will provide you with a valuable reference.

You might feel somewhat intimidated in the beginning and hesitant to bid; most everyone does. That feeling will disappear after you've had a chance to participate. Most tool auctions are "country style" and the atmosphere is friendly and informal. Naturally, it's better to attend your first auction with a knowedgeable auction-goer. He can fill you in on the procedures, the other participants, and the by-play and will soon have you bidding like a pro. But go, even if you have to go alone.

It's easy to be carried away at an auction, particularly if you're a competitive type. Two things to keep in mind:

1. Look carefully at each piece you plan to bid on during the preview before the auction and *don't bid on any item you haven't inspected.*

2. Fix in your mind (on paper is even better) what you are willing to pay for an item *and stick to it.* You may miss a few bargains, but you'll avoid a lot of mistakes.

Below is a list of the auctioneers who conduct periodic antique tool sales. Write and ask to be put on their mailing lists. There is usually a small charge for auction catalogs. Many allow mail bids.

- Brown Auction Services: 27 Medinah Drive, Flying Hills, Reading, PA 19607
- Christie's South Kensington Ltd.: 85 Old Brompton Road, London SW7 3LD, U.K.
- Barry Hurchalla: 343 High Street, Pottstown, PA 19464
- David Stanley Auction: Stordon Grange, Osgathorpe, Leicestershire, LE12 9SR, U.K.
- The Tool Chest: c/o Mike Jenkins, 1033 Crain Ave., Kent, OH 44240
- Your Country Auctioneer: c/o J. Lee Murray, Warner, NH 03278
- William Gustafson: P.O. Box 104, Austerlitz, NY 12017-0104 (entire auction is mail bid)
- Iron Horse Antiques: RD 2, Box 245-B, Pittsford, VT 05763 (entire auction is mail bid)

TABLE SALES (Preceding auctions)

This is the best place we know of to find 20 or 30 antique tool dealers all in one place, displaying their finest merchandise for sale. Most national tool auctions feature these sales in conjunction with the auction. These events are announced in the press, tool club periodicals, and in the flyers sent out by the auction houses.

CLUBS

We recommend that you join a local tool club and also one of the national tool societies. (See Clubs and Organizations, page 195). Even if you are not a joiner, a club's publication is worth the minimal annual dues. You'll also get valuable information from the meeting programs and from your fellow members. And you'll be able to swap, buy, (and sell, if you wish) at each meeting.

One last caveat: we suggest you be judicious in your use of price guides. No price guide can begin to cover the tremendous variety of tools that are available, or accurately reflect the wide diversity in price because of the variation in the condition of tools. And in a field developing as rapidly as antique tools, price guides can quickly go out of date. Guides do provide information that can be helpful, but you should appreciate their limitations.

In closing we repeat: there is no substitute for experience and knowledge, and that only comes with time and effort (and a fair number of mistakes). Fortunately, collecting antique tools is a fascinating and still unexploited field. That, and the many friendly and interesting people you will meet, will make the effort truly worthwhile.

BOOKS TO READ

Most of the books we list are being currently offered. However, those marked with an asterisk are out of print, but may be available at your local library. Astragal Press specializes in publishing books on antique tools and related subjects. Its address is P.O. Box 338, Morristown, NJ 07963-0338. A free booklist is available on request.

BOOKS OF GENERAL INTEREST

DICTIONARY OF WOODWORKING TOOLS, R.A. Salaman, Revised edition, 1989. Taunton Press, 63 So. Main St., Newtown, CT 06470. More an encyclopedia than a dictionary, this classic book describes and illustrates almost every imaginable variety of woodworking tool.

ANCIENT CARPENTERS TOOLS, Henry C. Mercer, 1975. Bucks County, PA, Historical Society, Pine St., Doylestown, PA 18901. A pioneering work on early tools, with particular emphasis on the American types.

*THE HISTORY OF WOODWORKING TOOLS, W.L. Goodman. G. Bell & Sons, 1964. The most comprehensive history of woodworking tools, beginning with the bronze age, through the Greeks and Romans, the middle ages, and up to the present time, complete with descriptions and illustrations.

BORING TOOLS

THE ULTIMATE BRACE, Reg Eaton. Erica Jane Publishing, 1989. Address: 35 High St., Heacham, Kings Lynn, Norfolk, England, PE31 7DB. A beautifully illustrated and carefully researched study of the Sheffield metallic framed brace, providing an insight into Victorian trade practices.

GUIDE TO AMERICAN BRACE PATENTS 1829-1910, Ronald W. Pearson, 1987. Available from the author: 1293 South Hill Road, Erie, PA 16509. A check list and brief description of approximately 400 early patented American braces.

EDGE TOOLS

*AMERICAN AXES, Henry J. Kauffman, The Stephen Greene Press, 1972. A well illustrated study of the development of the American axe, methods of production, and the various types that were made.

*AMERICAN AXE & TOOL CO. ILLUSTRATED 1894 CATALOGUE, reprinted by the Mid-West Tool Collectors Assn. and the Early American Industries Assn., 1981. Over 100 pages of illustrated axes and hatchets produced by the major manufacturer of the period.

BUCK BROS. 1890 PRICE LIST OF CHISELS, CARVING TOOLS, SCREWDRIVERS, AND PLANE IRONS. Reprint. Astragal Press. A 119- page catalog of one of the major edge tool manufacturers, illustrating and describing its line of edge tools.

PLANES

A GUIDE TO AMERICAN WOODEN PLANES AND THEIR MAKERS, 2nd Ed., E.& M. Pollak. Astragal Press, 1987. A complete guide to American planemakers. Over 1660 biographical entries, 1330 illustrated makers' marks.

BRITISH PLANEMAKERS FROM 1700, W.L. Goodman. Arnold & Walker, 1978; available from Astragal Press. The standard reference, providing invaluable information on the early 18th century planemakers, plus a comprehensive checklist of known British plane- and plane-iron makers.

WOODWORKING PLANES, A. Sellens, 1978. Available from the author, 134 Clark St., Augusta, KS 67010. A comprehensive description of plane types with emphasis on the mid-19th century major American manufacturers.

PATENTED TRANSITIONAL AND METALLIC PLANES IN AMERICA 1827-1927, Roger K. Smith, revised ed. 1990. Available from Astragal Press. The outstanding reference on the subject.

THE STANLEY PLANE, A. Sellens, 1975. Available from the author, 134 Clark St., Augusta, KS 67010. A history and descriptive illustrated listing of the Stanley tool line.

THE STANLEY CATALOG COLLECTION, Astragal Press, 1989. Complete reprints of the six most important 19th c. Stanley catalogs, the 1859, 1867, 1870, 1879, 1888, and 1898. Fully indexed; in one volume.

THE STANLEY COMBINATION PLANE, Kenneth Roberts. Astragal Press, 1989. Covers the development of the Stanley combination planes: the Miller, Traut, and Stanley 45 and 55. The planes are described and illustrated; patent information and, in the case of the 45 and 55, copies of the original instructions, are included.

THE COOPER AND HIS TRADE, Kenneth Kilby. John Baker, London, 1977. A book on coopering, by a cooper, that covers the methods and various tools used, including planes.

MEASURING TOOLS

BOXWOOD & IVORY: STANLEY TRADITIONAL RULES 1855-1975, Philip E. Stanley, 1984. Available from Astragal Press. Illustrates and describes the great variety of styles produced by the Stanley Rule & Level Co. and the manufacturing and marketing methods used.

JOHN RABONE & SONS: RULES & TAPES, 1892 catalog reprint, Kenneth D. Roberts 1982. Available from the author: P.O. Box 151, Fitzwilliam, NH 03447. A beautiful catalog that fully describes and explains the rule and level line of this pre-eminent manufacturer.

OTHER TOOLS

THE HAMMER: THE KING OF TOOLS, Ron Baird & Dan Comerford, 1989. Available from Dan Comerford, Box 271, Stony Brook, NY 11790. Provides hundreds of illustrations and information on approximately 200 American hammer patents.

ANTIQUE & UNUSUAL WRENCHES, Alfred & Lucille Schulz, 1989. Available from the authors: Rt.1, Box 151, Malcolm, NE 68402. A profusely illustrated study of wrenches, including many rare varieties.

CLUBS AND ORGANIZATIONS

One of the best and most enjoyable ways to learn more about tools is to join a tool group. Here you will meet other collectors who will share their knowledge and you will have an opportunity to see and to buy or sell or exchange all sorts of tools. You will also be able to share the enthusiasm and friendship of an interestingly diverse cross-section of society, young and old from all walks of life whose common interest transcends the usual social barriers. All the groups listed below welcome new members. Annual dues are generally modest.

NATIONAL ORGANIZATIONS

EARLY AMERICAN INDUSTRIES ASSOCIATION (EAIA)

The oldest (founded in 1933) and largest of the antique tool societies, it is international in scope. Members receive The Chronicle, a quarterly magazine on subjects relating to tools and collecting, and Shavings, a bi-monthly newsletter that lists meetings and events of interest to collectors. The Association offers members substantial discounts on relevant books and use of its library. It also sponsors an annual European tour for its members, visiting points of interest and meeting with foreign collectors and experts. Annual meetings are held around the country, often at well-known restorations, providing exhibits, lectures, seminars, tools sales and exchanges. Membership information can be obtained from John S. Watson, P.O. Box 2128, Empire State Plaza Station, Albany, NY 12220.

MID-WEST TOOL COLLECTORS ASSOCIATION (M-WTCA)

A very active group; despite its name it is national in scope. There are two meetings a year, at which there is much tool buying and selling and swapping, as well as exhibits and educational programs. This group frequently underwrites and distributes reprints of old tool catalogs and other interesting material. The M-WTCA has a number of affiliated regional clubs that also conduct meetings and swaps. Write to Morris K. Olson, 2825 Jackson Street, La Crosse, WI 54601.

SOCIETY OF WORKERS IN EARLY ARTS AND TRADES (SWEAT)

Emphasizes hands-on activities. Fred Bair, 606 Lake Lena Blvd., Auburndale, FL 33823.

TOOL GROUP OF CANADA

A well organized and active group that, as the name implies, specializes in Canadian tools and early agricultural, maritime, and industrial development. Stan Clarke, 112 Holmcrest Trail, Scarborough, Ontario M1C 1V5, Canada.

THE TOOLS AND TRADES HISTORY SOCIETY (TATHS)

This is the English tool society. It holds two meetings a year in such areas of interest as the Portsmouth Naval Yard and Iron Bridge. It publishes an excellent yearly journal and quarterly newsletter. Write to: The Secretary, TATHS, 275 Sandridge Lane, Bromham, Chippenham, Wiltshire SN15 2JW, U.K.

HAND TOOL PRESERVATION ASSOCIATION

This is the Australian tool society. Write to: John McDonald, 32 Rocklands St., Duffy 2611 A.C.T., Australia.

REGIONAL AND SPECIALIZED GROUPS

COLLECTORS OF RARE AND FAMILIAR TOOLS SOCIETY OF NEW JERSEY (CRAFTS)
Stephen Zluky, Box 243, Whitehouse, NJ 08888.

EARLY TRADES AND CRAFTS SOCIETY (LONG ISLAND, NY)
Steve Eckers, 11 Blyth Place, East Northport, NY 11731.

LONG ISLAND TOOL COLLECTORS ASSOCIATION (LITCA)
Ron Grabowski, 110 Burlington Blvd., Smithtown, NY 11787.

MID-ATLANTIC TOOL COLLECTORS ASSOCIATION
Richard Neilson, 1808 Fairfield Drive, Gastonia, NC 28054.

NEW ENGLAND TOOL COLLECTORS ASSOCIATION (NETCA)
Dorothy J. Sweatt, RR 1, Box 1000, Farmington, ME 04938.

OHIO TOOL COLLECTORS ASSOCIATION
George E. Woodward, P.O. Box 261, London, OH 43140.

PACIFIC NORTHWEST TOOL COLLECTORS (PNTC)
Steve Dice, 2267 S.W. 313th St., Federal Way, WA 98003.

POTOMAC ANTIQUE TOOLS & INDUSTRIES ASSOCIATION (PATINA)
Dave Clark, 8816 Rolling Acres Way, Olney, MD 20832.

PRESERVING ARTS & SKILLS OF THE TRADES ASSOCIATION (PAST)
Dave Paling, 227 Ney Street, San Francisco, CA 94112.

ROCKY MOUNTAIN TOOL COLLECTORS (RMTC)
Bill McDougall, 4020 Grande Drive N.W., Albuquerque, NM 87107.

SOUTHWEST TOOL COLLECTORS ASSOCIATION (SWTCA)
Troy Marshall, 224 Teak Lane, Streamwood, IL 60107.

THREE RIVERS TOOL COLLECTORS (WESTERN PA.)
Bob Kendra, 39 So. Rolling Hills, Irwin, PA 15642.

WESTERN NEW YORK ANTIQUE TOOL COLLECTORS ASSN.
Frank Kosmerl, 432 Hollybrook Road, Rochester, NY 14623.

MISSOURI VALLEY WRENCH CLUB
As the name indicates, wrenches are their bag, and they're a most enthusiastic group. Alfred W. Schulz, Rt.1, Box 151, Malcolm NE 68402.

INDEX